A New Similarity Measurement For Face Recognition

A New Similarity Photographic Measurement For Face Recognition

---

Tasaddi Mallak Hanon Al-Salih

and

Prof. Dr. Kadhim Mahdi Hashim

Preface

Gestures are one of the best ways of communication between dumbs and other people using the expression of signs language. In this book , we suggest an algorithm for recognizing hand gestures of Arabic (letters or numbers or words) to by using dumb (through signs) and convert the sings into voice corresponding to sings (letters or numbers or words). The proposed algorithm use video for gesture of the dumb then convert the video into frames (images), preprocessing for the resulted image must done by remove the noise, resize the images and increase the contrast, then calculate the distance to clustering the words by using (C4.5 , k-mean , k- medoid and artificial neural network), calculate the distance (or features) by using Euclidean distance and slope where ,there are eighteen features (eight features from Euclidean distance, eight features from slop, Area, and perimeter). The results in the training stage were (C4.5 gave 99.8664% , k-mean gave 97.7930%,k-medoid gave 97.3620%and ANN gave 96.538%). While in the testing stage we used three classifiers (Euclidian Distance, Modify of the Standardize Euclidian Distance and Correlation) and the results show that (Euclidian Distance gave 94.7368%,Modify of the Standardize Euclidian Distance gave 98.2456% and Correlation gave 96.4912%) We create our database (ten videos with 814 frames.

Declaration

Aware of legal liability I hereby declare that I have written this book myself and all the contents of the book have been obtained by legal means.

Author
Signature:
Date: / /2020
Name: Tasaddi Maalak Hanoun

ACKNOWLEDGEMENTS

Thanks are to our God for giving me health and desire to achieve this imperfect work and all what has been done, without his bless and support nothing can be done.

In addition, Above all, praise to Allah Almighty for His reconciliation. I would also like to thank my family and my friends for their unequivocal support, as always, for which my mere expression of thanks likewise does not suffice.

I would not possibly write this thesis without the help and support of the some people around me.

*This Dissertation would not have been possibly written without the help, support, advice and patience of my supervisor, **Prof. Dr. Kadhm .M.Hashim**. His experience, insightful comments and useful advice have decisively contributed to this work. The words, really, are not enough to express my gratitude for all what he does for me.*

The other important person I would like to thank my friend Zahoor Mosaad Edam for her help and support during preparing this Dissertation.

DEDICATION

I dedicate this thesis to the spirit

of My

father

and

brother

Who left me alone without a

farewell or hope to meet them

again

Tasaddi

Overview

Various image similarity assessment techniques can be used to detect differences between two images. In recent years, image similarity measure becomes an essential aspect in real world applications. It can be used for various image processing applications such as Recognition, dynamic monitoring, adjusting image quality, image enhancement, compression, restoration, and other applications. In this thesis, two new measures are proposed to measure the similarity between the two images. The first measure called MMDM, consists of two components. The first component is the Manhattan distance, which in turn depends on the geometric properties extracted from the image. While, The second component is the standard deviation of the properties extracted from the image, These two components are incorporated in a relative way . The second proposed measure is called MEDM; a modification of the measure known as the Euclidean Distance measure, by applying some mathematical facts to the measures to reach the best ratio of similarity that gives better results and closer to reality. The features extracted from the images are a hybrid type and the result is combining two types of features, the first type is geometric features and the second type is statistical features. The range of the measure lies between [0-1]. The proposed measures are tested with a noise type that Gaussian noise by using Mat lab R2014b and the face94 database that consist of 20 different images of 152 person , also used when the proposed measures are used for face recognition application.

The experimental results show that the proposed measures are compared with other existing and most popular similarity measures. The proposed measures (MMDM,MEDM) outperform existing measures (standard measures) SSIM , in detecting image similarity at low PSNR with Gaussian noise, with nearly 90_97% increase in performance.

Chapter Three: The Proposed algorithm

Chapter Four: Implementation and Results

Chapter Five: Conclusions and Future Works

References

Observed image X and saved images Y

List of Algorithms

Algorithms	Title	Page
Algorithm(1)	Pre-Processing Algorithm	40
Algorithm (2)	Geometric Feature Extraction	42
Algorithm (3)	SVD-Based Features Extraction (stored images)	43
Algorithm (4)	SVD-Based Feature Extraction (observed image)	45
Algorithm (5)	MMDM similarity measurement	48
Algorithm (6)	MEDM similarity measurement	52

List of Publications

- *Tasaddi MaalaK Hanoun And Kadhim M. Hashim* **"Modify Manhattan Distance For Image Similarity"** *," Open Journal of Science and Technology (OJST), 2019*

- *Tasaddi Maalak Hanoun And Kadhim M. Hashim* **"GEOMETRIC FEATURES AS A MEASURE OF FACES SIMILARITY"** *,Science Proceedings Series (SPS) journal,1(1) 2019.*

- *Tasaddi Maalak Hanoun And Kadhim M. Hashim* **"New Distance Measurements For Image Similarity,** *"Collage of Education for pure Sciences (JCEPS), 2019.*

Chapter One

General Introduction

1.1 Introduction

In image processing and computer vision measuring image similarity among two images is become a fundamental case in many problems [1]. In recent years, many images similarity measures were proposed, most of them work with very particular kind of image distortions [2].Some of them are viable to a wider range of applications such as the structural similarity measure (SSIM) index [3].

This chapter presents introduction to image similarity, similarity methods and explains the most related works in detail; also it presents a literature survey for image similarity measures.

1.2 Similarity

The similarity is the quality of the strong connection between two components of the database, while the difference deals with the measurement of the difference between two elemental data. The similarity scale ought to be inside 0 and 1 ,when similarity is one (exact similar) ,while the similarity is zero [4]. It also can be defined as the process of observing an image called X and a set of saved images called Yi as shown in figure(1.1). The saved images are given to determine the best matches of the saved images to the observed image [5,6]

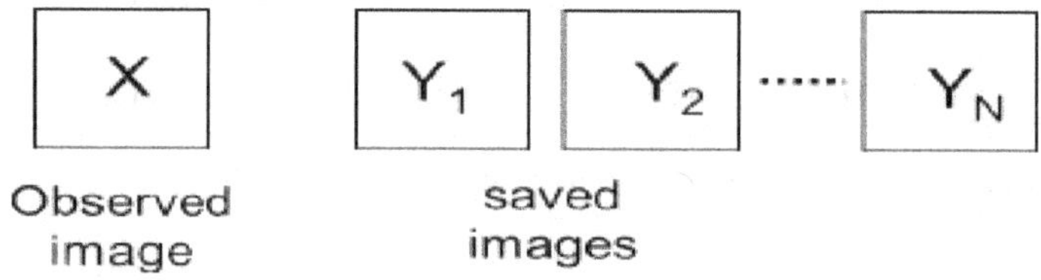

Figure (1-1)Observed image *X* and saved images

1.3 Similarity techniques

Numerous algorithms conform to facial and pattern   recognition systems. They are planned depending on the estimation of image similarity [8] .Image similarity scale techniques can be classified into: statistical and information theory [9].

1.3.1 Statistical based theory

Consideration and estimation data can be acquired from the image by calculating statistical measures, for example, mean, variance and standard deviation. This data can be utilized to calculate image similarity[10].

1.3.1.a Mean

The mean is the sum of all possible values that are weighted by the probability of that value [11]. It is formulated as

$$\mu_{A=\frac{1}{M}\sum_{i=1}^{M} A_i} \qquad (1.1)$$

where M is the number of values, A_i is the single value in the data set A .

1.3.1.b Standard deviation

Standard deviation can be defined as the measure that can be used to quantify the number of difference or dispersion of a set of data values [12] .

$$\sigma_A = \sqrt{\frac{1}{N-1}\sum_{i=1}^{N}(A_{i-}\mu)^2} \qquad (1.2)$$

where x represent a set of data values, N is the number of values and μ is the mean value of A.

1.3.1.c Structure Similarity Index Measure (SSIM)[13,14]

The SSIM is a full reference measure used to measure similitudes between two images. It can be considered as one proportion of the nature of the images being compared , given that the other images are viewed as the best quality. The similarity of structure consists of three comparisons: luminance, contrast, and structure . The main condition for luminance examination is exhibited as the follows:

$$L(A,B) = \frac{2\mu_A\,\mu_B + C_1}{\mu_A^2 + \mu_B^2 + C_1} \qquad (1.3)$$

Where

$$\mu_A = \frac{1}{M}\sum_{i=1}^{M} A_i$$

Where μ_A s the average of A, M is the number of values, A_i is the single value in the data set , is average of , c1= (k1L) L refers to maximum number of pixel values (255 for 8 −

bit grayscale images), and K1 is less than or equal one. The second equation for contrast comparison is as followes:

$$C(A,B) = \frac{2\sigma_A\,\sigma_B + C_2}{\sigma_A^2 + \sigma_B^2 + C_2} \qquad (1.4)$$

Where

$$\sigma_A = \sqrt{\frac{1}{N-1} \Sigma_{i=1}^{N}(A_{i-}\ \mu)^2}$$

where σ_A is Standard Deviation of A, A_i is the only value in the dataset, M is the number of values and μ_A is the mean of A , σ_B is Standard Deviation of B, σ_A^2 is variance of B, C2=$(K_2 L)$, is less than or equal one.

The third equation for structure comparison as following:

$$S(A,B)=\frac{\sigma_{AB}+C_3}{\sigma_A^2\sigma_B^2 C_3}$$

(1.5)

Where $C_3=C_2$ /2   Standard Deviation of two images calculate by two following equation:

$$\sigma_{AB}=\frac{1}{M-1}\Sigma_{i=1}^{M}(A_i - \mu_A)(B_i - \mu_B)$$

(1-6)

The final equation SSIM(x ,y) that is mixture of previous equations ((1.3), (1.4),(1.5)

$$SSIM(A,B)=[L(A,B)]^\alpha.[C(A,B)]^\beta.[S(A,B)]^\gamma$$

(1.7)

Where $\alpha,\beta,\gamma > 0$ These three criteria are used to determine how much importance to the equations previously mentioned, to simplify equation put values for each α,β,γ equal to one .

Get final equation SSIM as follows:

$$p(x,y) = \frac{(2\mu_A\,\mu_B + C_1)(2\sigma_A\,\sigma_B + C_2)}{(\mu_A^2 + \mu_B^2 + C_1)(\sigma_A^2 + \sigma_B^2 + C_2)} \qquad (1.8)$$

In general the structural of SSIM shown in Figure (1.2)

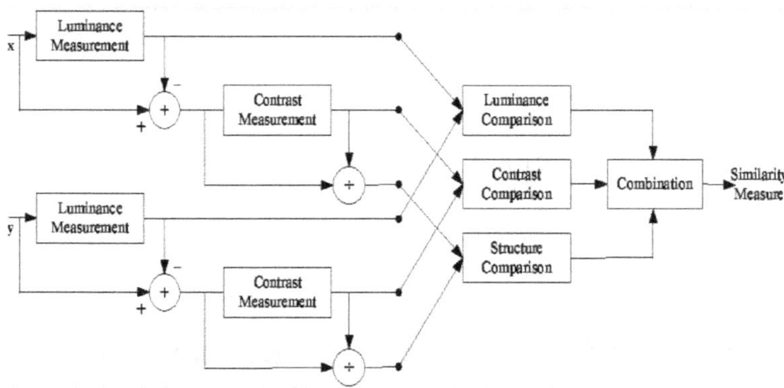

Figure (1-2)The structure of SSIM

1.3.2 Information Theoretic measure

Information-theoretic technique is the similarity measure for images. It aims to find the similarity between images according to their content (intensity values) [15]. These techniques are the most popular image similarity measures because they are able to predict the relationship between intensity values of an image [16].

1.3.2.a Mutual Information

Mutual information (MI) can be defined as the measure of the mutual dependence among two random variables (RV) [17]. Since MI expresses the amount of information that variable contains about variable as mentioned in Eq(1.9) [18]

$$MI(A,B)=H(A)+H(B)-H(A,B) \qquad (1.9)$$

Where H(A),H(B) are the marginal entropy of A and B respectively and their joint entropy. If and are two RVs then MI is given as follows [19]:

$$MI(A,B) \ = \sum_{A,B} P_{A,B}\,(A,B)\log\ \frac{P_{x,y}(A,B)}{P_A(A).P_B(B)}$$

(1.10)

Where, $P_{A,B}(A,B)$ is the joint probability distribution function of the two RVs and $P_A(A)$ and $P_B(B)$ are the marginal probability distribution functions of the two RVs respectively.

1.4 Similarity Applications

Image similarity can used for various image processing applications as follows

1- Recognition: Object Recognition when Object Detection followed Object Identification and other applications .

*2- **Dynamic monitor:*** It is part of the full Dynamic Elements bundle and allows you to display picture frame .

*3 - **Adjust image quality**:* Adjustment layers give additional editing flexibility.

*4 - **Enhancement**:* The principal objective of image enhancement is to process a given image so that the result is more suitable than the original image for a specific application.

*5 - **Compression**:* The problem of reducing the amount of data required to represent a digital image. • This means from a mathematical viewpoint: transforming a 2-D pixel array into a statistically uncorrelated data set.

*6 - **Restoration:*** The purpose of image restoration is to restore a degraded/distorted image to its original content and quality[8].

1.5 Criteria quality

The process of determining the level of accuracy is called Image Quality Assessment (IQA),which is part of the quality of experience measures. Image quality can be assessed using two methods: subjective and objective. Subjective methods are based on the perceptual assessment of a human viewer about the attributes of an image or set of images, while objective methods are based on computational models that can predict perceptual image quality [20].There are many cretiria quality such as the follows:

1.5.1 The Mean-Squared Error (MSE)

In statistics, the mean squared error (MSE) or mean squared deviation (MSD) of an estimator (of a procedure for estimating an unobserved quantity). It can be considered as one of the simplest and oldest image similarity assessment methods [21,22]. MSE has been the predominant quantitative performance measure in the domain of signal processing. MES remains the standard criterion for the valuation of signal quality; it is the best method for comparing signal processing methods and systems [23]. MSE in physic has often a clear meaning as the energy of the error signal, which is defined as the difference signal between two compared images.

MSE can be defined as the average of the squared errors, which mean the difference between the estimator value and what is estimated [24].

1.5.2 Peak Signal To Noise Ratio(PSNR)

PSNR is the proportion between the most extreme conceivable intensity of a sign and the intensity of adulterating commotion that influences the nature of its portrayal. Since many signs have a wide unique range, (proportion between the biggest and littlest potential estimations of an alterable amount), the PSNR is normally communicated regarding the logarithmic decibel scale[25].

$$PSNR = 10.\log_{10}\left(\frac{MAX_X^2}{MSE}\right) \qquad (1.11)$$

where, MAX x is the maximum possible value of pixel of the image. Note that if x is the gray image of 8-bit representation for each sample .

MAX x$= 2^8 - 1 = 255$

1.6 Biometrics

One emerging technology that becomes more prevalent in such organizations is biometrics. To make a personal confession, Biometrics depends on somebody's identity or what he does in contrary to what he knows (like the password) or what he has (such as an ID) [26].

Biometrics refers to the unique physiological features (facial, fingerprints and ear) and behavioral traits (keystrokes, sound and walking dynamics) of individuals that can be used for the identification or verification purposes.

On the other hand, biometric techniques are capable of confronting such threats: the biological characteristics of people cannot be misplaced or difficult to forget, and difficult to steal or create Passwords and PINs are vulnerable to attacks of loss, theft and guesswork. Similarly, magnetic cards are subject to loss, theft, forgery and duplication[27].

1.6.1 Requirements of Biometric Systems

The biological and behavioral requirements have requirements that are met by these requirements[28].Every person should use the application should have its own advantage.

A.Universality: Every person should use the application should have its own characterizes.

B.   Uniqueness (Distinctiveness): Different characteristics of different people are   important enough to exist.

C .Permanence: During a certain time these properties must be   fairly constant .

D. Measurability (Collectability): By devices we can get the required characteristics .

E. Performance: The identification tool must indicate and under certain limitations to accuracy and repetition .

F. Acceptability: People accept to use such techniques

G. Circumvention: The Use of fraudulent methods to easily fool the system such as (fake fingers, physical traits and mimic behavioural traits).

1.6.2 Types of Biometric

Although there are many ways to use biometrics to identify someone, they all fall into two classes (see figure (1.3)) : physiological and behavioural [14]:

1.Physiological Category: Relevant to the body shape (for examples: face discrimination, fingerprint, hand geometry, and iris discrimination).

2.Behavioral Category: Relevant to the person's behavior manner (examples: signature and voice).

Biometrics in Early Stages include DNA, Retina recognition, Thermo grams, Gait, Keystroke ,

Ear recognition , Skin reflection, Lip motion and Body order [29].In figure (3.1)has been explained the last types of the biometrics categories .

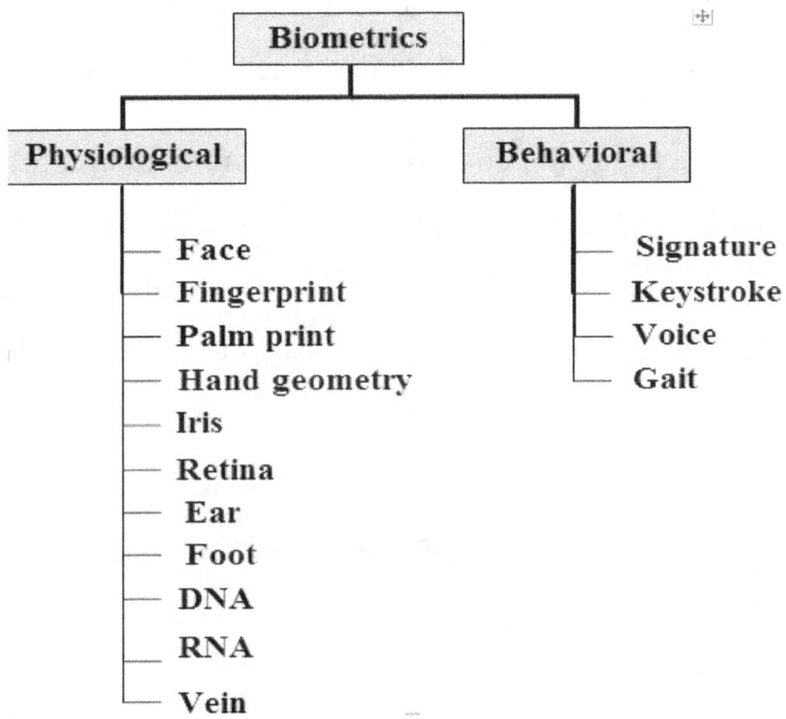

Figure (1.3) physiological and behavioural biometric[30]

1.6.3 Biometric Identity By Face

The usually used biometrics have many problems. Iris recognition is very accurate, but costly for operation on a wide scale and is not very accepted by people. As for fingerprints, the disadvantage is the lack of cooperation by people, but for its advantages, it is very reliable. At present, face recognition appears to be a good compromise between reliability and social getting which balances security and isolation well. Facial recognition techniques work almost freely in terms of unrestricted acquisition conditions as well as their ability to deal with large numbers of unaware people .So, Facial recognition technology is becoming the most popular biometric techniques [29].

There is a study considering the compatibility of six biometric techniques (face, finger, hand, voice, eye, signature) with Machine Readable Travel Documents (MRTD) facial features counted the highest ratio of compatibility, as explained in Figure (1.4). In this study, parameters like the enrolment, regeneration, mechanism requirements and public view are considered [31].

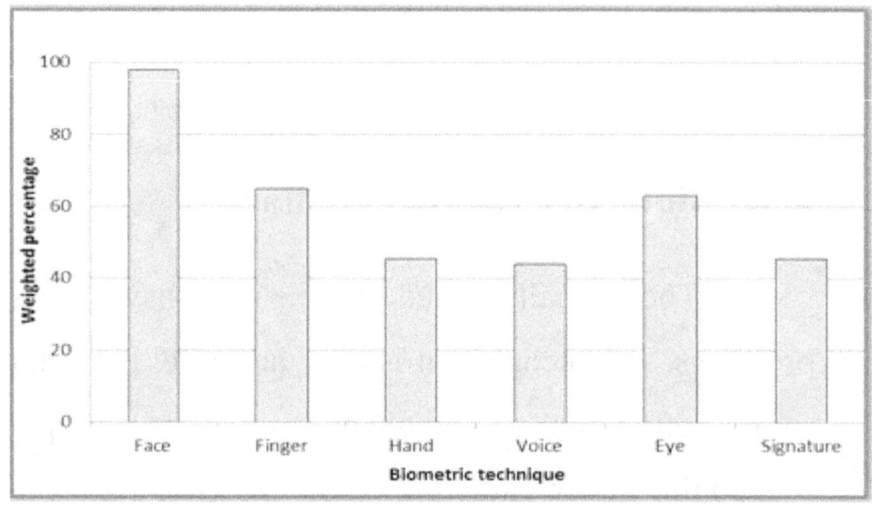

Figure (1.4):A comparison of various biometric features based on MRTD compatibility [30]

One key advantage of a facial recognition system is that it is able to person mass identification as it does not require the cooperation of the test subject to work. Properly designed systems installed in airports, multiplexes, and other public places can identify individuals among the crowd, without passers-by even being aware of the system.[31]

However, as compared to the other biometric techniques, face recognition may not be most reliable and efficient. Quality measures are very important in facial recognition systems as large degrees of variations are possible in face images. Factors such as illumination, expression, pose and noise during face capture can affect the performance of facial recognition systems.Among all biometric systems, facial recognition has the highest false acceptance and rejection rates,[34] thus questions are raised regrading the effectiveness of face recognition software in cases of railway and airport security.[32]

1.6.4 A common face recognition system

A face recognition system consists of four parts: detection, pre-processing, feature extraction, and matching. Face recognition (facial feature extraction and matching) is performed after localization and normalization (face detection and Pre-processing) are processing steps .These parts are explained in figure(1.5):

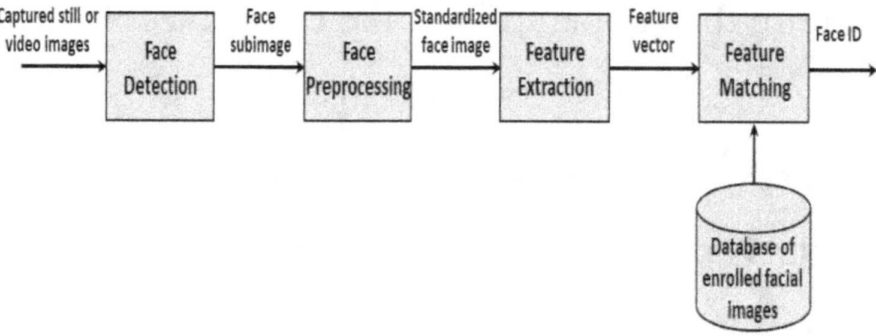

Figure (1.5): The four common steps in face recognition system [30].

The details of the steps are explained in the next chapter.

1.6.5 Applications of Face Recognizing

The accompanying applications are utilized in the Face Recognition [32,33]as follows:

1. **ID and verification**: facial recognizing can be utilized for both confirmation and recognizable proof. Apple introduces Face ID on the flagship iPhone X as a biometric authentication successor to the Touch ID, a fingerprint based system[34]

2. **Access control**: in a large number of the entrance control applications, for example, access to the workplace or signing into a PC, the extent of the gathering of individuals requiring acknowledgment is moderately little. The images of the face are caught in

common circumstances, for example, inside illumination and frontal faces. The facial recognition system of this application can accomplish high accuracy.

3. Recognizing of the database of images, like The path to input dataset of face images. pursuit of datasets categories of missing youngsters, foreigners, authorized drivers and police holds.

4. Security: it is a significant viewpoint in airplane terminals, aircraft staff workplaces and explorers. It contains face images organized into subfolders by purpose. Facial recognizing innovation is utilized in air terminal security frameworks that have been completed in numerous airplane terminals around the world. As of late 2017, China deploye facial recognition and artificial intelligence technology in Xinjiang. Reporters visiting the region found surveillance cameras installed every hundred meters or so in several cities, as well as facial recognition checkpoints at areas like gas stations, shopping centers, and mosque entrances.[35]

5. Reconnaissance: observation through face recognition systems s has a low dimension of client fulfillment. The arrangement of facial acknowledgment frameworks for observation is a difficult undertaking because of facial introductions, lighting situations s, etc.

In addition Face recognition systems are also used by photo management software to identify the subjects of photographs, enabling features such as searching images by person, as well as suggesting photos to be shared with a specific contact if their presence were detected in a photo.[36]

1.7 literature review

Numerous scholars introduce the measure of similarity with different approaches. Some of these works are shown below:

Z. Wang and A. Bovik (2004), the researchers introduced a method for quality assessment that based on the degradation of structural information. They develop a structural similarity index. They proposed measure that is called SSIM by using combination of statistical parameter such as mean, variance and standard deviation. SSIM is proposed to improve the traditional quality assessment methods such MSE and PSNR [22].

Jassim T. Sarsoh (2012) , they classifying the human face images based on the graph theory concepts. They propose an effective clustering algorithm. The principle idea of this algorithm depends on the graphic theory by using the definitions and terms of the graph and the tree. Automatic algorithm are used it does not need to give the number of the resulted clusters a priori. In this research project is the algorithm depended on value of threshold. The changing in this value effects results for each cluster, causing a decrease in the efficiency of this algorithm, in addition to that there are some cases that cause low in the efficiency of the algorithm as follows, face images for more than one person are lied in same cluster. Alternatively, the face images of some person were partitioned in two clusters. This occurred when they use a big value for the constant threshold[37].

M. P. Sampa and Z. Wang (2009), the researchers introduced an image similarity measure, which is called complex wavelet structural similarity (CW-SSIM) index, and then they showed that it can be used as a multipurpose image similarity index. There are some advantages of CW-SSIM index, firstly it stand against translations and small rotations, secondly it"s provides useful comparisons in spite of missing of the pre-processing image registration step [38].

H. Wang, D. Maldonado, S. Silwal, (2011), the researchers proposed a new similarity measure. They proposed measure replaces the correlation and contrast comparisons of SSIM and based on test of independence nonparametric hypothesis between the error signal and the compared images [39].

D. Mistry, A. Banerjee and A. Tatu (2013), the researchers, proposed a new similarity measure that is based on joint entropy (joint histogram). The measure of uncertainty among two images, so if the joint entropy is low, the similarity between two images are high and vice-versa. The joint entropy is applied on two compared images using joint histogram [5].

A. F. Hassan, D. Cai-lin and Z. M. Hussain (2014), the researchers proposed an information-theoretic method for structural similarity for estimate the gray scale image quality. This paper presents an image similarity measure that is called HSSIM. Information–theoretic technique that is based on the concept of joint histogram which is used to provide useful comparisons in spite of missing of the pre-processing image registration step [40].

F..M. mahmood ,H. R. Mohammed and Z.M. Hussainy.(2017) , the researchers proposed a new similarity measure that is called SjhCorr2 (Symmetric Joint Histogram— 2-D correlation) which is a hybrid measure that is based on both: information-theoretic and statistical based . The proposed measures are tested under different noise type such as Gaussian noise and impulsive noise .[7]

Z.M.Aydam and S.K.Ali 2019, the researchers proposed a new similarity measure that is called modify Standardize Euclidian distance (Gestures conversion to Arabic letters)[41].

1.8 Research problem

Image similarity measures today becomes an essential point in real world application since it can be used in a lot of image processing applications such as dynamic monitor and adjust image quality, enhancement, compression, restoration, recognition, etc. Changing demands and changing criteria, make researchers think ,how to propose new robust measure for image similarity that robust under low peak signal to noise ratio (PSNR) rather than enhance the existing measures such as SSIM which failed under significant noise.

1.9 The Aims and Objective

The main aim of this research is to propose new similarity measurement   deals with some face recognition problems such as facial expression change, illumination change, multi-poses as frontal, etc. The objectives of thesis are detecting of similarity between two images automatically for image quality assessment ,and studying the statistical and geometric features that are based mainly on HVS of images.

1.10 Contributions

In this thesis we contribute to the following points: .

1. Proposing new hybrid measure that based on statistical and geometrical   features.

2. Proposing new measures that based on geometrical based only.

3.Using traditional Manhattan ,Euclidian distance to proposed new measure.

1.11 Thesis Organization

In addition to this chapter, the thesis consists of four other chapters, which:

Chapter Two: This chapter gives theoretical background of similarity measures and face recognition system.

Chapter Three: This chapter shows the design and implementation steps of the proposed system, and the description of all algorithms that are used to implement the proposed system.

Chapter Four: This chapter contains the main datasets which are used in the thesis, and , the test results which are presented and discussed to evaluate the performance of the established system.

Chapter Five: This chapter contains some derived conclusions which are listed of and a list suggestions for the future works which is give

Chapter Two

Theoretical Background

2.1 Introduction

Dependence on pixel color only does not give good results in measuring similarity. So, we rely on the properties of the image to be more secure plus the color tone of the pixel[43].

2.2 Facial recognition system

Facial recognition system is a technology capable of identifying or verifying a person from a digital image or a video frame from a video source. There are multiple methods in which facial recognition systems work, but in general, they work by comparing selected facial features from given image with faces within a database. It is also described as a Biometric Artificial Intelligence based application that can uniquely identify a person by analyzing patterns based on the person's facial textures and shape[44].

2.3 Face Recognition Methods

Recognition algorithms can be divided into two main approaches as follows:

1.geometric, which looks at distinguishing features, or

2.photometric, which is a statistical approach that distills an image into   values and compares the values with templates to eliminate variances.

Some classify these algorithms into two broad categories that contain recognition of input pickle files. If you are working with own dataset, you can store the output recognizing manager files here as well.[45] The output files include:

1. **Holistic Matching Methods**:

   They try to identify the face in its entirety and the zone of the face is considered as information into the face catchy system. Eigen faces , Principal Component Analysis, Linear Discriminant Analysis using the Fisher face algorithm and independent component analysis , are instances of the holistic methods..

2. **Feature-based Methods**:

   The feature-based partition into works such as according to features and evaluate each in addition to its spatial location with feature to other features[46] extraction of local features,

for example, nose, eye and mouth, their statistics and locations are fed into a classifier. The "restoration" is an extraordinary test for feature- based methods . Local Feature Analysis (LFA), the Elastic Bunch Graph Matching (EBGM using the Fisher face algorithm), and so on are instances of Feature-based methods. The various strategies for tree extraction are [47]:

a) Generic based on lines, edges, and curves.

b) Feature-template-based methods.

c) Structural matching methods.

3. Hybrid Methods:

Hybrid discernment systems utilize a mix of both holistic and feature based methods.The 3D system continues along these lines: Detection, Position, Measurement, Representation and Matching.

2.4   Problems with Face Recognition:

1. **Orientation Problem**: .Turnover of image may be differed with relation to camera optical axis, and this be automated face recognition a difficult task [5]. An example of pose variation is shown in figure(2.1)

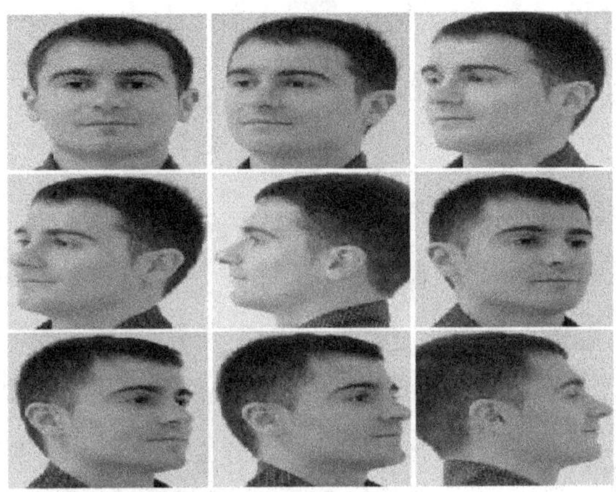

Figure(2.1) orientation in face [5]

2. **Occlusion problem:** the faces in the images may be partially occluded by some objects. For example, the presence of glasses, beards or a person standing in front of another (illustrated in Figure(2.2) [45]

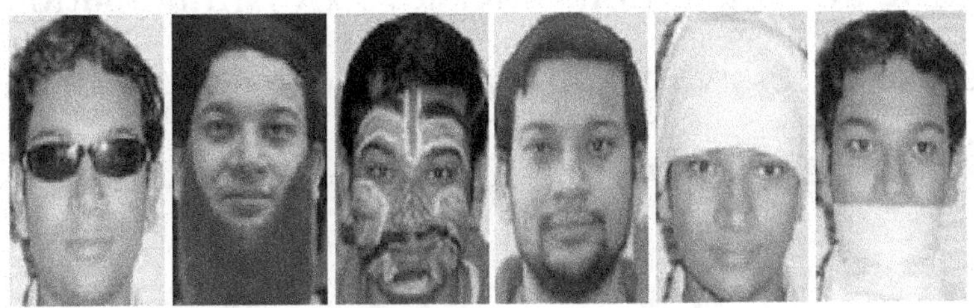

Figure (2.2): Occlusion Variations in Human Face [45]

3. Face Expression problem:

Facial expressions can be a basis problem when differentiating unknown faces. The expression can affect the appearance of the face (illustrated in Figure 2.3) [48].The faces of people change from moment to moment. Even in the course of a conversation with someone, changes are seen in their expressions and in the angle of their head.

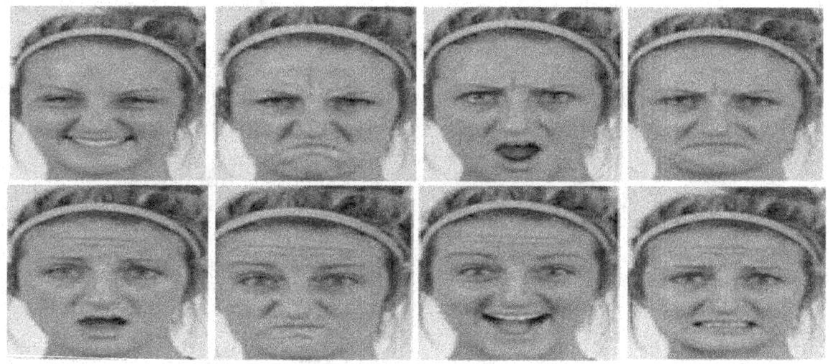

Figure (2.3): Changes in facial expressions[48].

4. Illumination problem:

different lighting situations can affect the speed of discernment. Low levels of illumination in the front or bottom make the detection and recognition of the face much more difficult, in addition, high levels of illumination can cause excessive facial exposure (illustrated in Figure 2.4) [44].

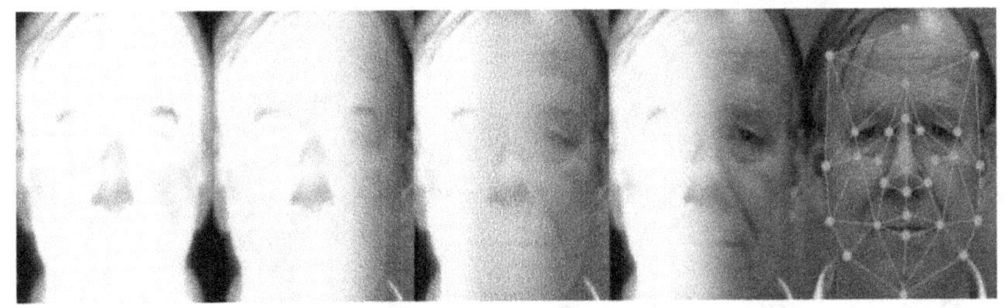

Figure (2.4) Variations of the Illumination on the human face.[44]

5.Aging of the face: Another reason for the changes in the facial disguise could be due to the aging of the face and could affect the automatic facial recognition process (demonstrated in Figure 2.5) [49].

Figure(2.5) Age variation in human face.[49]

6. Image size: When a face detection algorithm discovers a face in an image or in a video frame, the relation size of that face matches with the registered image size changes how well the face will be accepted [50]. (see Figure 2.6)

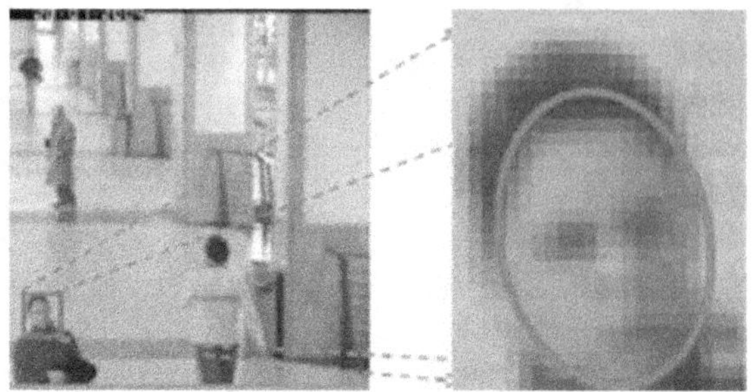

Figure (2.6): Small size face region[50]

7. Inter-Class Similarities: Differentiating between two identical twins is not difficult but still at times a hard work straight for their parents (see Figure 2.7).This is a challenge for biometric technologies .But it also challenges humans brains. It is the problem of distinguishing between two different issues that have very similar features. In many cases, multi-biometric methods like relating face and fingerprint recognition develop the performance [51].(see figure 2.7).

Figure (2.7): Inter-Class similarity of frontal faces between twins[52]

2.5 Region of Interest Image Geometry

Often, for image analysis, we want to investigate, more closely specific area within the image called Region of Interest(ROI).To do this need operations that modify special coordinates of the image and these are categorized as image geometry operations. The image geometry operations discussed here include crop, zoom, enlarge, shrink, translate and rotate.

The image crop process is the selection of portion of the image ,sub image and cutting it away from the image. Once we have cropped sub image from the original image. We can zoon in on it enlarging it. Image enlargement is useful in a variety some applications since it can help visual analyses of detail object.[53].

2.6 Face detection

The human face is defined in digital images by computer technology used in many applications. Psychological condition can be determined by the face detection process and can be brought in a visual scene(((is a computer technology being used in a variety of applications that identifies human faces in digital images. [54]Face detection also refers to the psychological process by which humans locate and attend to faces in a visual scene[55],for example,

Open CV's technology is based on the Viola-Jones method in face exploration. It was discovered in 2001. It explores all the objects in the image, containing the portions of the face. We collect the portions of the face to be the face of a somebody and review in four points:

1. Haar features represent a simple rectangle.

2. For early detection of shapes and faces, we implement image integration.

3. We use the Ada Boost theory for machine learning .

4. We work the association of face parts (nose-eyes mouth) using a cascaded classifier to be image[54] .The theory of Viola-Jones method depends on on transforming Haar wavelets into image exploration. One square wave is Haar wavelets ,one high or one low part, and 2D displacement a square wave involving pairs of nearby rectangles each with two black and white colors as in the following :

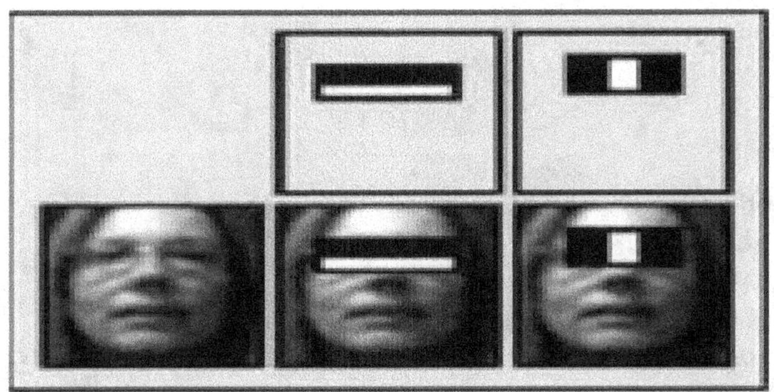

Figure(2.8) The first two Haar features in the original
Viola-Jones cascade[54]

In order to obtain the HAR rate, we subtract the sum of the pixel values in the black area from the total pixel values in the white areas and the result is divided by the total pixels in the two regions ,by the threshold agreed upon in the theory of learning if the result of the difference is higher than that of. This part of the face and is searches the other parts in the same box .Integral integration is a way to group small parts together and the last is pixel values . The sum of each pixel is the integral values for pixel that falls over it. (A + B + C + D) The value of pixel in position 3 is A + C,and the pixel value in position 2 is A + B. The value of pixel in position 1 is in (A).(see Figure 2.8)

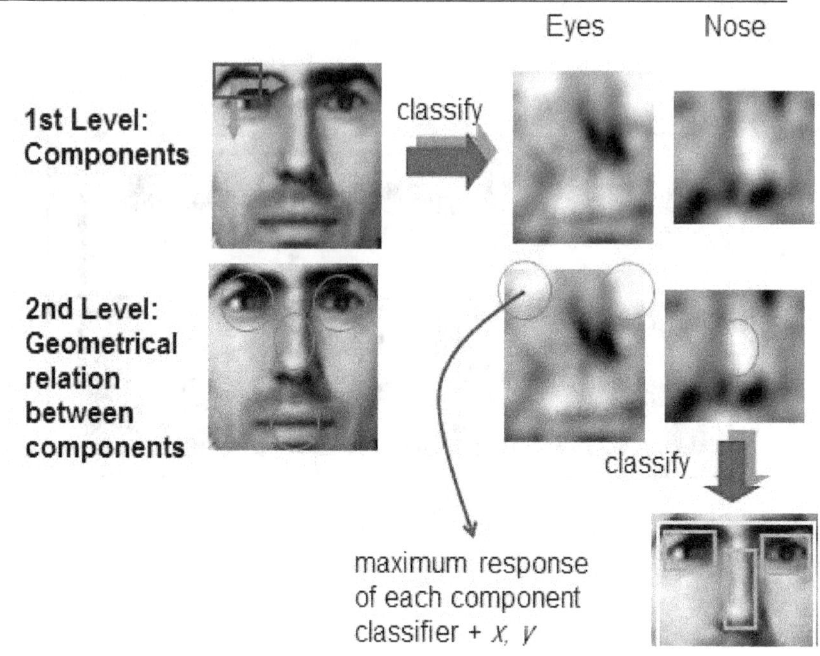

Figure (2-9) Component-based Detection[54].

2.7 Feature extraction

At this stage and after the implementation of appropriate pre-processing, the main features are extracted .These features are powerful against pose, illumination, expression and aging differences [56].There are two type of features can be described by the following:

2.7.1 Geometric features

Geometric features are the features of the objects that are created by a group of geometric elements like points, lines, curves or surfaces. In our proposed Algorithm, there is a set of geometric measurements

(Euclidean distance, Slope, Area, Perimeter, Centroid and Extreme Points, Angle and Rotation) to extract the features of the human face   as better than the others; the mathematical description of these measurements is given below:

2.7.1.a Euclidean distance

It is the distance   between two points in Euclidean space. $P_1(x_1, y_1)$ and $P_2(x_2, y_2)$ are in two-dimensional alphanumeric spaces[57]

If $P_1(x_1, y_1)$, $P_2(x_2, y_2)$ are two points, then the Euclidean Distance between P_1 and P_2

is given b

$$EU(P_1, P_2)$$
$$= \sqrt{(x_1 - x_2)^2 + (y_1 - y_2)^2} \qquad (2.1)$$

then, eq. (2.17) can be generalized by defining the Euclidean distance between P_1 and P_2 as

if the points need n dimensions, such as p=(x_1, x_2, ...,x_n) and P =(y_1,y_2 ,...,y_n) then, eq. (2.16) can be general by defining the Euclidean distance P_1 between and P_2 as

$$EU(V, P) =$$
$$\sqrt{(v_1 - p_1)^2 + (v_2 - p_2)^2 + \cdots + (v_n - p_n)^2} \quad (2.2)$$

for explain that can you see Figure (2.10)

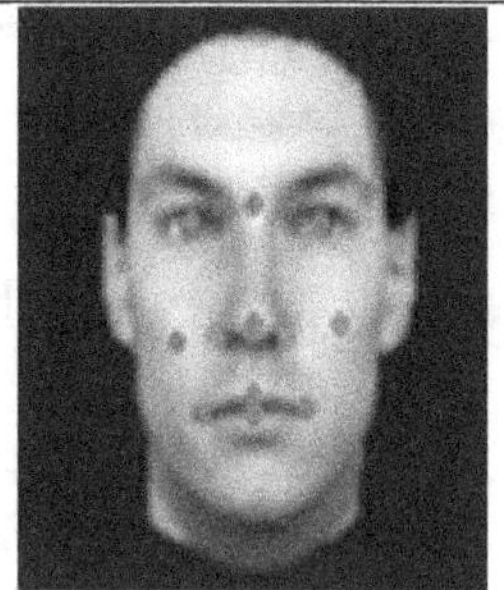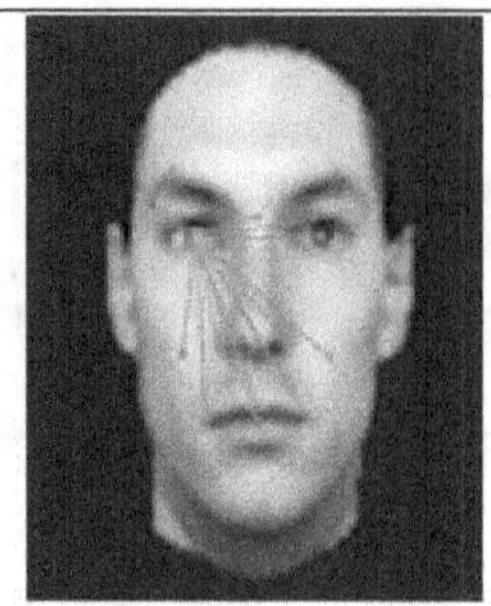

Figure (2.10)display how Using Models of Pair-wise Positions[57]

2.7.2.b Slope

The straight line is   a set of points that which has a fixed slope between any two points. The slope of the straight line is usually determined by the value of the ratio of vertical change to horizontal variation. The slope usually describes the slope of the two-point line. The parallel line of the x-axis is defined as the horizontal line, Zero. The parallel line of the y-axis is known as the vertical line, and its slope always has an undefined value. The parallel two lines always have

slope equal [58].This is described by the following equation(2.3).

$$Slope = \frac{yz-yo}{xz-xo} \qquad (2.3)$$

2.7.1.c Area

The area is an extension of shapes, which is different from the ocean. As it is linked within the shape, there are many known formulas for simple shapes such as triangles, rectangles and circles. Using these formulas, any polygonal region can be calculated by dividing the polygon into triangles or circles to obtain curved shapes with borders and then compiling them after calculating their regions. When the polygon is irregular, the polygon region can be calculated by the trapezium Gauss equation and described as in the following equation(2.4)[58]

$$Ar = \frac{1}{2}\sum_{i=0}^{m-1}(x_{ii} * y_{ii+1}) - (x_{ii+1} * y_{ii}) \qquad (2.4)$$

m: number of points

x_{ii}=axis coordinates

y_{ii}=axis coordinate

2.7.1.d The Perimeter

The Perimeter is the length of the line that encompasses the two-dimensional shapes, for example, the circle, square, square shape or sporadic shapes. The Perimeter can be determined as in equation (2.5) if the shape is symmetrical while the

equation (2.6) calculates the perimeter if the shape is ribbing inequilaterally [59].

$$Prm = m * (A) \qquad (2.5)$$
$$Prm = \sum_{i=0}^{m-1} A_i \qquad (2.6)$$

where $\qquad$ m: Number of ribs

A:length of the rib

2.7.1.e Centroid and Extreme point

The centroid is a fixed point in the object where the lines go through this point which speaks to the weight of the object. The centroid is unique in relation to one another as far as structure or acclimatization and subsequently decide the status of a centroid identified with this distinction. The centroid can be determined by the accompanying equation(2.7)[60].

$$x_a = \frac{\sum x_{ai} A_{ii}}{\sum A_{ii}}, \ y_a = \frac{\sum y_{ai} A_{ii}}{\sum A_{ii}} \qquad (2.7)$$

where:

x_a: the - axis value when center point of shape

y_a: the - axis value when center point of shape

x_{ai}: The distance at which the center of the shape be far from the junction point of the axes on axis (x).

y_{ai}: The distance at which the center of the shape is far from the junction point of the axes on axis (y)

A_{ii}: area the shape.

While Extreme point is "(8*2) matrix that limits the extreme points in the region. Each row of

the matrix has the x- and y-coordinates of one of the points. The format of the vector is (right-top, right-bottom, left-top, left-bottom ,top-right, top-left, bottom-right and bottom-left). This may be is supported only for 2-D input label matrices".

2.7.1.f Angle

Is the separation or break between the two straight lines merging with one another, where the crossing point of the two lines and their intersection are known as the angle head (Vertex), and the two lines the two parts of the angle are known know two of the angle, The angle comprises two bars going from a similar beginning stage. The angle determines any between the two intersectional lines According to the accompanying equation (2.8)[61]

$$Angle = tan^{-1}((S_1 - S_2)/(1 + S_1 * S_2))$$

$$(2.8)$$

S_1 : The slope between (Y) and (X).

S_2 : The slope between (Y) and (Z).

2.7.1.g Rotation

The rotation converts over a pixel esteem from a original image to another situation in the pivoted image by turning it at a clockwise point around the first. The rotation can be performed utilizing the accompanying equation (2.9) [62]:

$$\left. \begin{aligned} &= q * cos(\theta) - Q * sin(\theta) \\ \hat{q} &= q * sin(\theta) + Q * cos(\theta) \end{aligned} \right\}$$

$$(2.9)$$

Where:

(q, Q) and ($\hat{p}\,\hat{q}$) : are pixel coordinates before and after rotation, respectively,

θ: is the counter clockwise angle of rotation

2.7.2 Singular Value Decomposition

Singular value decomposition (SVD) is a decent strategy to extricate image features .It has invariance for the turn and reflecting change, and furthermore has better heartiness for clamor and light force change [63]. SVD is the result of direct polynomial math. It plays an intriguing, key job in a wide range of uses that is, face recognition, image compression, watermarking, object detection, scientific computing, signal processing, texture classification and so on [64]. The singular value decomposition of a matrix is one of the most elegant the most rich and amazing calculations in straight polynomial math, and it has been widely utilized for rank and measurement decrease in example pattern recognition and information retrieval applications [65].

To characterize the SVD, it is helpful first to characterize eigenvalues and eigenvectors. On the off chance, A will be a square matrix, of size nxn and λ is a related eigenvalue with the end goal that:

$$Au_i = \lambda_i u_i \qquad (i = 1,2, \dots, n) \qquad (2.10)$$

Then, u is called an eigenvector of matrix A, associated with eigenvalue λ. The above equation can be rewritten as:

$$Au_i = \lambda_i I u_i \qquad (2.11)$$

where I is the characteristic matrix of size nxn. The extent of this identity matrix has to be the same as that of the matrix for which the eigenvalues and eigenvectors have to be calculated. Equation (2.11) reduces to

$$(A - \lambda I)\, u = 0 \qquad (2.12)$$

The eigenvalues λ of matrix A are those real numbers for which the homogeneous system defined by equation (2.12) has a non-zero solution and the eigenvector of matrix A associated with λ is the non-zero solutions of this system. Equation (2.12) has a non-zero solution if its coefficients' matrix is

41

noninvertible and this is possible if its determinant is equal to zero, for example

$$|A - \lambda I| = 0 \qquad (2.13)$$

The equation (2.13) is said to be the characteristic equation of matrix A.

SVD is based on the following theorem of linear algebra, whose proof is beyond our scope. Given an $m \times n$ matrix, X, there exist square unitary matrices U and V of dimensions $m \times m$ and $n \times n$, respectively, so that [66,67]:

$$X = USV^T \qquad (2.14)$$

And

$$S = \begin{bmatrix} \Lambda^{\frac{1}{2}} & 0 \\ 0 & 0 \end{bmatrix} \equiv U^T X V \qquad (2.15)$$

where $\Lambda^{\frac{1}{2}}$ is the $r \times r$ diagonal matrix with elements $\sqrt{\lambda_i}$, with $r \leq \min\{m, n\}$ (r is equal to the rank of X) , and λ_i , $i = 0,1, \dots, r - 1$, are the r nonzero eigenvalues of XX^T , which are similar with the eigenvalues of $X^T X$, and $\sqrt{\lambda_0} \geq \sqrt{\lambda_1} \geq \cdots \geq \sqrt{\lambda_{r-1}} \geq 0$ are known as the singular values of X. 0 denotes a zero element matrix. T is the transpose operator as matrices U and V are unitary and orthonormal matrices ($UU^T = I$ and $VV^T = I$, where I is the identity matrix).

The columns of the orthogonal matrices U and V are called the left and right singular vectors respectively. In other words, there exist unitary matrices U and V that transform X into the singular diagonal structure of S . Equivalently, we can write

$$X =$$

$$[u_0 , u_1 , \dots , u_{r-1}] \begin{bmatrix} \sqrt{\lambda_0} & & & \\ & \sqrt{\lambda_1} & & \\ & & \ddots & \\ & & & \sqrt{\lambda_{r-1}} \end{bmatrix} \begin{bmatrix} v_0{}^T \\ v_1{}^T \\ \vdots \\ v_{r-1}{}^T \end{bmatrix}$$

$$(2.16)$$

Or

$$X = \sum_{i=0}^{L-1} \sqrt{\lambda_i} \, u_i v_i{}^T \qquad (2.17)$$

where $u_i , v_i , i = 0,1, \dots , r - 1$, are the corresponding eigenvectors of XX^T and X^TX, respectively. Moreover, u_i and v_i , $i = 0,1, \dots , r - 1$ are the first r column vectors of U and V, respectively. The rest of the column vectors of U and V corresponds to zero eigenvalues. If we retain $L \leq r$ terms in the summation of Eq. (2.18), that is,

$$\hat{X} = \sum_{i=0}^{L-1} \sqrt{\lambda_i} \, u_i v_i{}^T \qquad (2.18)$$

then $\widehat{X}$ is the best approximation of X of rank L.
See figure (2.4).

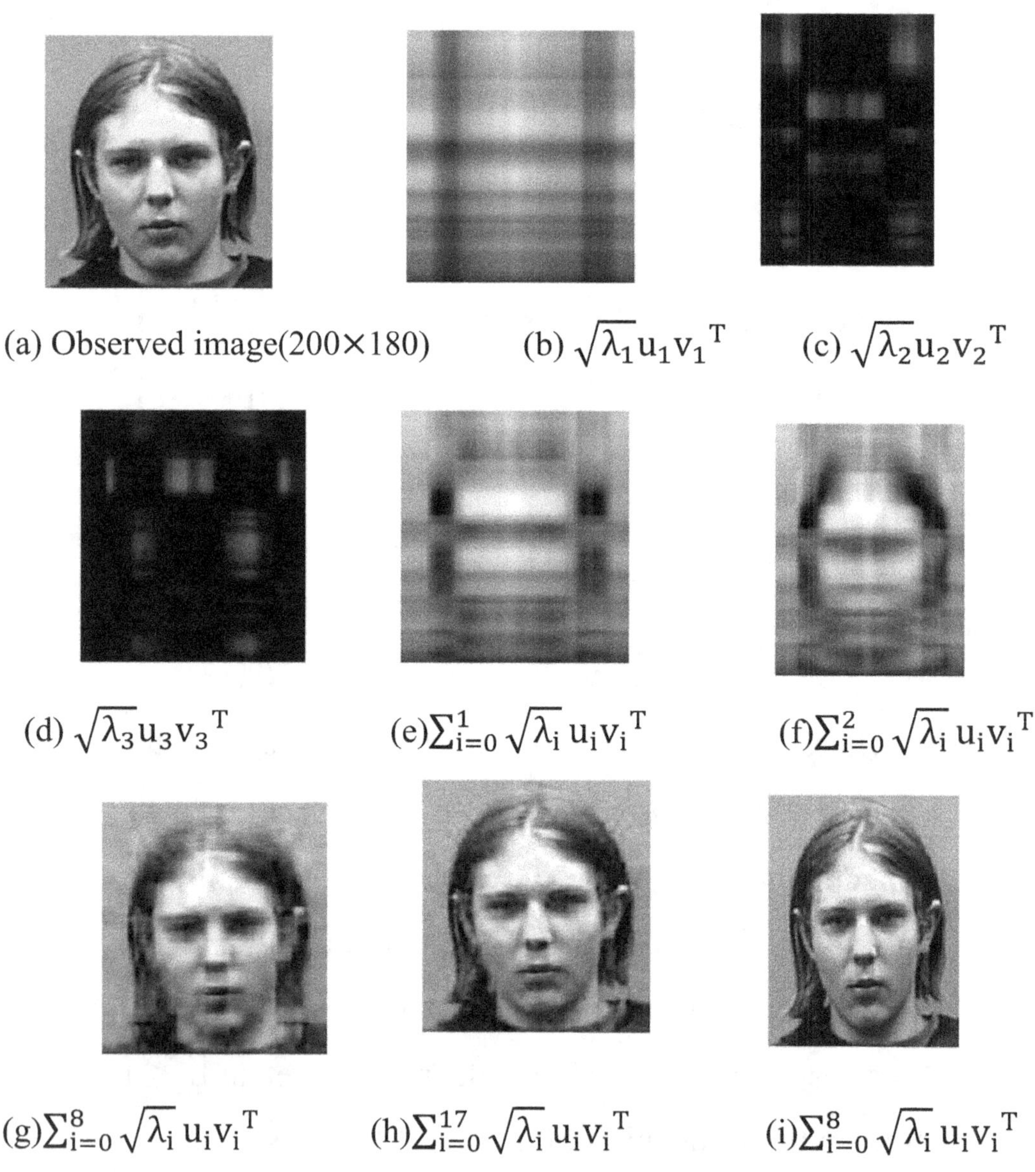

(a) Observed image(200×180) (b) $\sqrt{\lambda_1}u_1v_1{}^T$ (c) $\sqrt{\lambda_2}u_2v_2{}^T$

(d) $\sqrt{\lambda_3}u_3v_3{}^T$ (e)$\sum_{i=0}^{1}\sqrt{\lambda_i}\,u_iv_i{}^T$ (f)$\sum_{i=0}^{2}\sqrt{\lambda_i}\,u_iv_i{}^T$

(g)$\sum_{i=0}^{8}\sqrt{\lambda_i}\,u_iv_i{}^T$ (h)$\sum_{i=0}^{17}\sqrt{\lambda_i}\,u_iv_i{}^T$ (i)$\sum_{i=0}^{8}\sqrt{\lambda_i}\,u_iv_i{}^T$

Figure (2.4): (a) Original image (b), (c), (d), (e) , (f), (g),
(h) and (i) are approximations of the observed image

Some mathematical properties of SVD are [68]:

a) SVD can be performed on any real m×n matrix.

b) The singular values are unique, while the matrix U and V are not unique.

c) $XX^T = USV^T(USV^T)^T = USV^TVSU^T = US^2U^T$

hence V diagonlises X^TX. It follows that the matrix V can be computed through the eigen vector of X^TX.

d) The matrix U can be computed through the eigen vector of XX^T.

e) The rank of the matrix X is equal to the number of its non-zero singular values.

Additionally, SVD has the accompanying significant properties of a picture : dependability, transposition invariance, turn invariance, extent invariance and mirror change invariance. In [67], these significant properties were demonstrated. The SVs highlight vector of the facial picture contains minimal helpful data for face acknowledgment and most significant data is encoded in two symmetrical matrices of SVD [68].

2.8 Fusion Methods

Fusion (combination) is simple and economical to improve recognition performance. The goal of fusion is to get a higher accuracy than each individual classifier or feature vectors. The premise of fusion is that different classifiers or features can overcome the drawbacks of each other [69].

In general, there are four methods for fusion: Simple sum, Append, Weighted sum and Multiplication .

Let D_A and D_B to be two distance vectors which result from A-Based and B-Based Features Extraction. Combine the two resulting vectors D_A and D_B in order to find the combined vector D_{Fusion}[70].

a) **Simple Sum :** In this case D_{Fusion} is calculated as the mean of the two distance vectors D_A and D_B .

$$D_{Fusion} = \left(\frac{(D_1^A + D_1^B)}{2}, \frac{(D_2^A + D_2^B)}{2}, ..., \frac{(D_M^A + D_M^B)}{2} \right) \qquad (2.19)$$

where M is number of training images.

b) Append: In this case, D_{Fusion} is calculated as the Append of the two distance vectors D_A and D_B .

$$D_{Fusion} = (D_1^A, D_2^A, ..., D_M^A, D_1^B, D_2^B, ..., D_M^B)$$

$$(2.20)$$

c) Weighted sum : In this case D_{Fusion} is calculated as the weighted sum of the two distance vectors D_A and D_B .

$$D_{Fusion} = ((w_A \times D_1^A + w_B \times D_1^B), (w_A \times D_2^A + w_B \times D_2^B), ...,$$

$$(w_A \times D_M^A + w_B \times D_M^B))$$

$$(2.21)$$

where w_A and w_B are the weights associated to the classifiers A or B respectively.

d) Multiplication : In this case, D_{Fusion} is calculated as the Multiplication of the two distance vectors D_A and D_B .

$$D_{Fusion} = ((D_1^A . D_1^B), (D_2^A . D_2^B), ..., (D_M^A . D_M^B))$$

$$(2.22)$$

2.9 Similarity Functions

Based on the features derived from the image, we can determine the similarity measures. When the target range is [0,1] , the similarity function is referred to as a dichotomous similarity functional. To make it clear, it can be said that the methods described above which are used to calculate distances are all used in the situation of binary attributes; whereas the nominal

attributes are not seen as distances but rather as similarity functions.

In this thesis, two measures are used for the similarity. The first is the modification of the Euclidean distance and the second is the modification of the distance of Manhattan. These two measures are tested and the best proportion of the known measurements was obtained. In Chapter three, we explain in detail these functions are explained in chapter three.

2.10 Distance Measures

A further advance ought to be thought about to the extent bunching of information that is the gathering of similar objects. To show up similarity, one more advance of estimation is required. Two fundamental sorts of estimations are found to evaluate this connection; the first is the distance measure. To make it obvious, utilizing distance measures for some bunching techniques to choose whether a pair of objects is similar or dissimilar; it is crucial and important to determine the distance of two instances x_i and x_j $d(x_i, x_j)$. The legitimacy of distance measure can appear by its being symmetric also, it ought to acquire on account of indistinguishable vectors its base esteem which is constantly zero. On the off chance that the distance measure fulfills explicit properties, as appeared in Eq.

(2.12) and Eq. (2.13) individually, at that point, it is known as a measurement remove [71].

There are different distances are used in this thesis can be explained in the following:

1 .Euclidean distance

As shown in the section **2.6.1**

For example,   if xx=(aa, bb) and yy=(cc, dd) the Euclidean distance between xx and yy is

$$EUD = \sqrt{(aa - cc)^2 + (bb - dd)^2}$$

$$(2.1)$$

2.City block distance or-Manhattan :

Take the sum of the absolute values of the differences of the coordinates.[69]

For example, if xx=(aa ,bb) and yy = (cc ,dd) the Manhattan distance between xx and yy is

$$D_{ctb} = \sum \ |(aa - cc) - (bb - dd)| \qquad (2.23)$$

For your vectors, it is the same thing except if you have more coordinates.

A taxicab geometry is a form of geometry in which the usual distance function or metric of Euclidean geometry is replaced by a new metric in which the distance between two points is the sum of the absolute differences of their Cartesian coordinates. The taxicab metric is also known as rectilinear distance snake distance, city block distance,

Manhattan distance or Manhattan length, with corresponding variations in the name of the geometry[72]. The latter names allude to the grid layout of most streets on the island of Manhattan, which causes the shortest path a car could take between two intersections in the borough to have length equal to the intersections 'distancein taxicab geometry. .(see Figure 2.12)

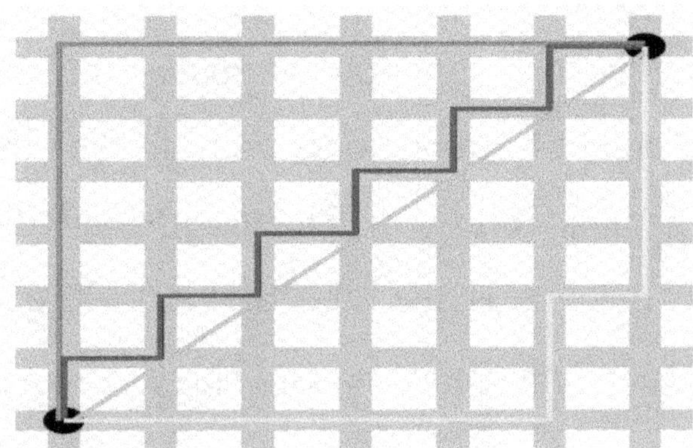

Figure (2.12) display Graphical comparison between Manhattan and Euclidean distance[72]

In Figure (2.12)We have Taxicab geometry versus Euclidean distance: In taxicab geometry, the red, yellow, and blue paths all have the same shortest path length of 12,while in Euclidean geometry, the green line has length and is the unique shortest path.

The properties for Taxicab distance depend on the rotation of the coordinate system, but do not depend on its reflection about a coordinate axis or its translation. Taxicab geometry satisfies all of Hilbert's

axioms (a formalization of Euclidean geometry) except for the side-angle-side axiom, as two triangles with equally "long" two sides and an identical angle between them are typically not congruent unless the mentioned sides happen to be parallel. Also ,the Manhattan distance function computes the distance that travel to get from one data point to the other if a grid-like path is followed. The Manhattan distance between two items is the sum of the differences of their corresponding components[73].

The formula for this distance is between a point X=(X1, X2, etc.) and a point Y=(Y1, Y2, etc.) is:

$$\sum_{i=1}^{n} |X_i - Y_i|$$

Where n is the number of variables, and Xi and Yi are the values of the ith variable, at points X and Y respectively.(see Figure 2.13)

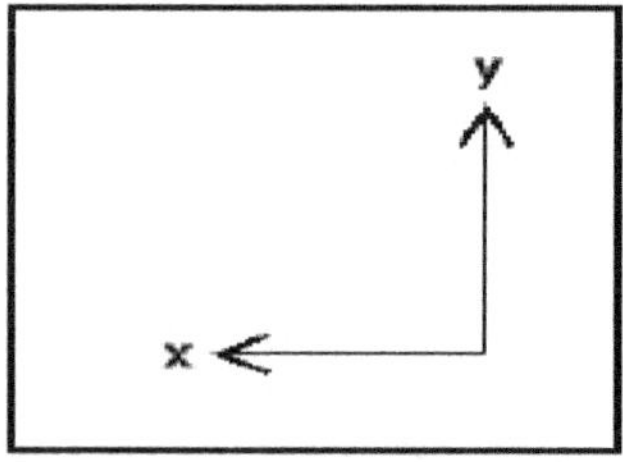

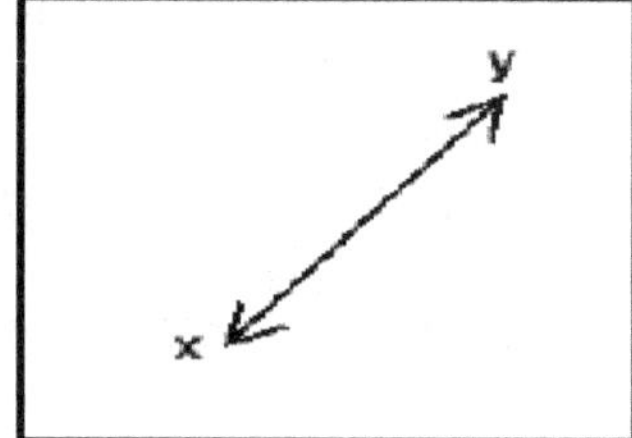

Manhattan

Euclidian

Figure (2.13) illustrates the difference between Manhattan distance and Euclidean distance[73]

4. Minkowski distance

Given two p-dimensional instances, pi = (pi1, pi2, ... , pip)and pj = (pj1, pj2, ... , pjp),the distance between two object instances can be calculated using the Minkowski method as explain in equation(2.23) [71].

$$DMW\ (i, j) = ((pi1 - pj1)2 + (pi2 - pj\ 2)2 + \cdots + (pip - pjp\ )2)1\ p\ (2.24)$$

4. Che bychev distance

"Chessboard distance", formalized as Chebyshev distance, is a metric defined on a vector space where the distance between two vectors is the greatest of their differences along any coordinate dimension as explain in equation (2.25) [72].

$$DCb(x, y) = maxi{=}1,2,...,\text{m}\ |pi - qi\ |$$

(2.25)

2.11 Image Noise

Common noise represents the unwanted things produced in the image [74]. Image noise is random difference of brightness or color information in images. Noise can be created from dissimilar sources such as the sensor and circuit board of a scanner or digital camera. Image noise can also create in film grain and in the necessary shot noise of an ideal photon detector. Image noise is an unwanted by-product of image capture that increases false and minor information [17].

2.11.1 Noise Type

Normal images are degraded with additive noises displayed with either a Gaussian, or impulse noise (salt and pepper) distribution. Another normal noises are a speckle noise, which is multiplicative in nature and Poisson noise [75].

a. Gaussian Noise

Gaussian noise is squarely distributed above the signal [76]. Generally each pixel in the noisy image is values of the sum of the a random Gaussian distributed noise and true pixel.

The probability distribution function takes the shape of the bell as such .

$$PG(x)=\frac{1}{\sigma\sqrt{2\pi}}\,e^{-\frac{(x-\mu_x)^2}{2\sigma^2}}$$

(2.26)

where x signifies the grey level, σ the standard deviation and.

μx the mean value.

b. Impulse Noise (Salt and Pepper Noise)

Fat-tail distributed or "impulsive" noise is at times called salt-and-pepper noise or spike noise The image that has noise of this type has white pixels in the dark region and vice versa. Digital analog converter errors and transmission errors are one of the reasons for this type of noise.

In an image consisting of 8 bits, the salt is 256, but the pepper is close to zero. These values are damaged in the pixels of the original image. As for the unaffected units, they remain as they are .Some of the causes of this noise are timing errors in digitization, faulty memory locations, or pixel faults in camera sensors[77].

C. Poisson Noise or noise is a type of electronic noise that occurs when the narrow number of units that transfer vitality, for example, electrons in an electronic circuit or photons in an visual device, is little enough to run a growth to facts that can be famous by differences In appreciation [76]

D. Noise of the mantle:

The noise of the mantle is a double noise which occurs in almost all coherent imaging systems, such as lasers, acoustics, and synthetic aperture radar images. The source of this

noise is due to the random interference of coherent returns. The fully developed noise noise is characterized by double noise [77].

Chapter Three

The Proposed Methods

3.1 Introduction

The general scheme and plan of the proposed face recognition framework is illustrated in figure (3.1).The proposed system is divided into two phases, the first is comparison of similarity that is created on stored and experiential spitting image and the second is recognition face that based is on which are training phase and testing phase. The training phase is a process of training the input database to classify the face sample. The testing phase is used to classify the face sample based on the training phase.

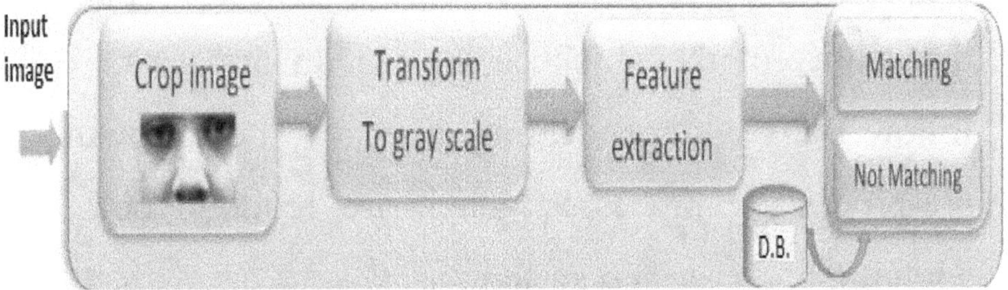

Figure(3.1) general scheme proposed method

3.2 The Proposed System

The stages of the proposed face recognition system are explained in the following subsections:

3.2.1 Read Image

Read image from graphic file and return image data in an array. The system accepts any type of image (image format :BMP,JPEG, PNG, GIF, WebP, BPG, etc).

3.2.2 Image Pre-Processing

To evaluate the quality of the quantized images a subjective quality test is used in which a number of face recognition is enquired to criticize the quality of the sequence images. To estimate the quality of the quantized images, a subjective quality test is used in which a number of face themes are requested to judge the quality of the sequence images. In our tests, we follow the recommendations given by the following pre-processing processes which are required before applying the projected system:

a) Cropping image: In order to additional reduction in memory consumption and computational complexity, we obtain the images in database to NxM (the size 48*50 is used in our experiments).

b) Convert Image to Gray scale: Convert the color image to the gray scale intensity image.

c) Convert all faces (stored and observed) into double type to simplify mathematical operations.

<table>
<tr><td>Algorithm(1): Pre-Processing</td></tr>
<tr><td>Input:
Image //any image, may be stored x , or observed y</td></tr>
<tr><td>Output:
Image after Pre-Processing</td></tr>
<tr><td>Begin
Step 1:-crop image into NxM (48*50) is used in our experiments).
Step 2:- Convert image into a gray scale.
Step 3:- Convert image values into double type.
End Algorithm</td></tr>
</table>

Figure (3.2): Represent Pre-Processing algorithm

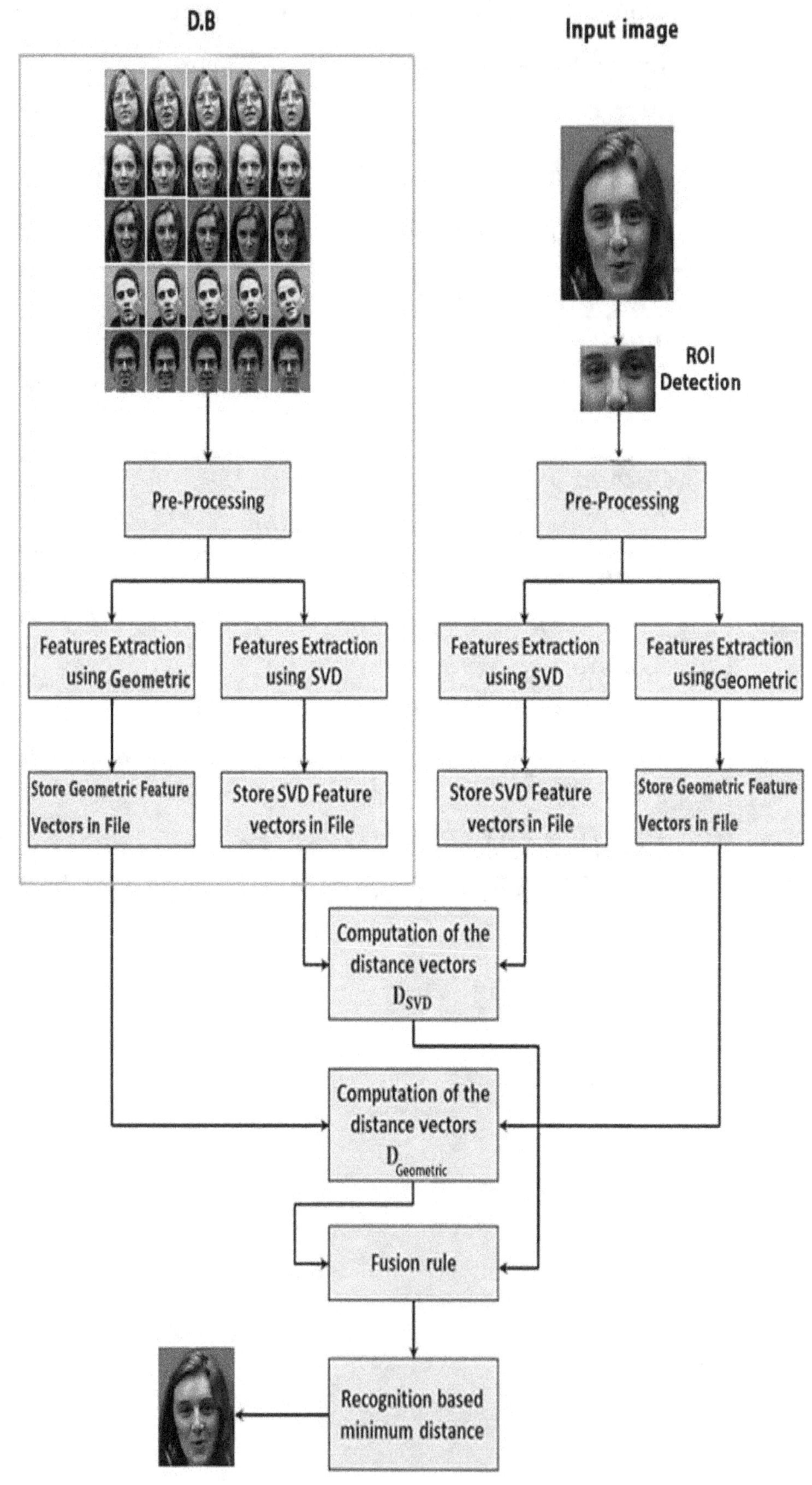
D.B
Input image
ROI
Detection
Pre-Processing
Pre-Processing
Features Extraction using Geometric
Features Extraction using SVD
Features Extraction using SVD
Features Extraction using Geometric
Store Geometric Feature Vectors in File
Store SVD Feature vectors in File
Store SVD Feature vectors in File
Store Geometric Feature Vectors in File
Computation of the distance vectors D_{SVD}
Computation of the distance vectors $D_{Geometric}$
Fusion rule
Recognition based minimum distance

Figure (3.3): Block diagram of proposed face recognition system

3.2.3 Feature Extraction

Our proposed measure similarity is based on the main two types of features that represent the geometrical and statistical ,they which are shown below.

3.2.3.1 Geometric-Based Features Extraction

In our proposed calculation, there are 14-geometrics highlights for each (image). These 14 features are isolated into two sets; the main set is comprises of (12- features) from figuring the separation between the four point, the subsequent set additionally incorporates (2- features) from ascertaining the edge between eye center focuses with point face focus and edge between eye focus focuses with point nose center.(see Figure 3.4)

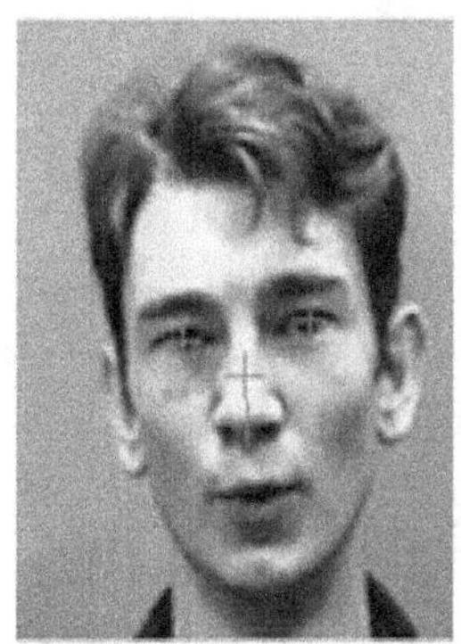

Figure(3.4) shown the position of points in face

Algorithm (3.2) gives the steps for this operation.

<table>
<tr><td colspan="1">Algorithm (2): Feature Extraction</td></tr>
<tr><td>Input : gray level image</td></tr>
<tr><td>Output : Features Extraction</td></tr>
<tr><td>

Begin
Step1: Extract 4 points of face.
Step2: Calculating the 12-features contain the distance of 4 points by using the Euclidean distance from the each to others according to equation (2.1) as figure(3.4).
Step3: Calculate 2-angle between three themes as according to equation (2.7)
Step4: Feature extraction as vector [distance   angle].
end

</td></tr>
</table>

Figure (3-5) algorithm for extraction geometric feature

3.2.3.2 SVD-Based Features Extraction

To offer a better accepting of the SVD in image processing and find many important applications and open research pieces advices in important areas increasingly; SVD independent image processing in the coming study. Since SVD has a difference for the mirroring reflecting change and rotation, and furthermore develop vigor for light power change and commotion, so this technique is used to extract the massive and critical image features . As mentioned in chapter 2 section (2.7.1) SVD has three matrices (U

(the   left singular vectors) , S (the singular values) , V (the right singular vectors)) . The left and right solitary vectors of face images include a lot of data than the specific qualities and they can provide a higher response rate. Hence , we utilize left and right solitary vectors .

The SVD-Based Features Extraction structure put away images and image test is depicted in Algorithm (3) and Algorithm(4), respectively. See figure (3.6) and Figure (3.7).

Algorithm(3): SVD-Based Features Extraction (saved images)
Input: I // face images

Output:
        Fsvd // Fsvd is SVD features vectors for saving images.
        SU   // SU is the first U_{col} columns from left singular vectors
        SV   // SV is the first V_{col} columns from right singular vectors

Begin

Initialization: U_{col}=7 , V_{col} =3 , Fsvd = [ ], Γ=[]   //   Fsvd , Γ are   an empty vectors

Step One:- Pre-Processing for SVD-Based Features Extraction

For (i = 1; i <I) do

x = Retrieve image i

x=Pre-processing on image x using **Algorithm(1) .**

x=convert   image   into   column vector((N*M)X1).

Γ =[Γ x]   //Eq.(2. 3) store all columns vector in matrix.

end loop

Step Two:- Compute the mean of images from   the   **following** instruction:

$$Mean = \frac{1}{I}\sum_{i=1}^{I} \Gamma_n \qquad ((N*M)X\ 1))$$

//Eq.(2.4)

where I is No. of images in storing set

Step Three: Mean2= Reshape the mean image   array   (Mean)   into   (N*M) **is used in our experiments).**

$Mean2 = reshape(Mean')'$;   //   by   using reshape   function

of   MATLAB, where   '   is transpose function of MATLAB

Step Four:- Compute SVD of the mean image(Mean2) **from** **the** **following instruction:**

$[U\ S\ V] = svd(Mean2)$ //Eq.(2.17) , svd

is Singular value

decomposition

function of MATLAB

Step five:-

SU = **Select first U$_{col}$ columns from U matrix**

SV= **Select first V$_{col}$ columns from V matrix**

Step six:- Compute Features Extraction

For (i = 1; i <I) do

x = Retrieve image i

tp = SU ^{t} * x * SV   (U$_{col}$* V$_{col}$) // Eq.(3.1)

tp = convert image (tp) into column vector   ((U$_{col}$* V$_{col}$)X 1).

Fsvd = [Fsvd tp] // store all Fsvd vectors in matrix.

end loop

End Algorithm

Figure (3.6): Represent SVD-Based Features Extraction storing images) algorithm

In this section, the proposed method is described briefly. Four sets of features are extracted one in the spatial domain and three in the frequency domain. The first set is extracted based on the SVD feature extraction method proposed in the feature vector is obtained for every image. Then, the same algorithm is performed to extract the features of number of investigations which are directed by extricating the element vectors for various number of left and right solitary vectors (U col, V col), however best outcomes are acquired for the qualities (U_{col}=7,

V_{col} =3). Total features are (U_{col} * V_{col} =7*3=21 features)

<table>
<tr><td>Algorithm(4): SVD-Based Feature Extraction (observed image)</td></tr>
<tr><td>

Input:

      y   //   y is observed image

      SU   //   SU is first U_{col} columns from left singular   vector

          created by **Algorithm(2)**

      SV   // Select_V is first V_{col} columns from right   singular   vectors

          created by **Algorithm(2)**

</td></tr>
<tr><td>

Output:

      Tsvd //   Tsvd is   SVD feature vector for observed image .

</td></tr>
<tr><td>

Begin

    Step One:- Pre-Processing for SVD-Based Feature Extraction

        y = Retrieve image y

        y=Preprocessing on image y using **Algorithm(1)** .

    Step Two:- Compute Feature Extraction

        Tsvd = SU ^{t} * y *   SV (U_{col}* V_{col}) // Eq.(3.1)

End Algorithm

</td></tr>
</table>

Figure (3.7): Represent SVD-Based Feature Extraction (observed image) algorithm

3.3 Similarity Measure

The performance of the proposed framework when it is required to confirm the personality of one individual utilizing face images enlisted at various ages is genuinely great, considering that the variety of face images is in various vectors. In geometric-Based

Features Extraction, we have a vector v of size V which contains the highlights relating to the watched face and a lattice of models U,(U=[u1 ,u2,u3,..u14) of size , (U×M) such as M represents the number of store faces, each column of U is a model vector of an individual of the face database. Where the first elements are the distances and the last two elements are the angles. The comparison between U and v is done by calculating the distances between v and each column of U, so we obtained a distance vector D which represents the score to be combined with SVD.

In SVD-Based Features Extraction, we have a vector v of size $(U_{col}*V_{col})$ which contains the features corresponding to the test face and a matrix of the models U , $(U = [u_1, u_2, ..., u_M])$ of size $((U_{col}*V_{col})\times M)$ such as M represents the number of stored faces, each column of U is a model vector of an individual of the face database. U_{col} is the first 7 columns from left singular vectors, V_{col} is the first 3 columns from right singular vectors. The comparison between U and v is done by calculating the distances between v and each column of U, so we obtained a distance

vector $D_{SVD} = (d_1, d_2, ..., d_M)$ which represents the score to be combined with geometric.

In our study, we distance measurement; this measurement is described in Algorithm(6), see figure (3.9) .

A number of global and local methods are available for the representation of face images, but no single approach is found to be suitable in most of the situations. As the information conveyed by these two feature sets, is different; hence, the techniques that combine the global and local features together are necessary to obtain the optimal results. In this thesis, we develop an approach to combine two feature sets obtained from SVD and geometric approaches. SVD approach is able to efficiently represent the global variations of face images whereas the geometric is one of the most useful descriptors to extract the local variation of face images. In order to analyse the effectiveness of the proposed approach obtained by the fusion of SVD and $D_{geometric}$ approaches, various experiments are carried out on SVD and $D_{geometric}$ face databases. The proposed approach is also been compared to some existing techniques and from the detailed experiments it has been observed that the

results obtained by the proposed method are far better than these approaches.

3.4 The Fusion Strategy

As mentioned in chapter 2 section (2.7.2), there are four methods for fusion, the append method is used in our experiments because it gives better results than other methods when we combine Geometric and SVD.

Let $D_{geometric}$ and D_{SVD} be two distance vectors which result from Geometric-Based and SVD-Based Features Extraction. Combine the two resulting vectors $D_{Geometric}$ and D_{SVD} in order to find the combined vector D_{Fusion} .

We calculate D_{Fusion} as the append of the two distance vectors $D_{geometric}$ and D_{SVD}

$$. D_{Fusion} = \left(D_1^{Geo}, D_2^{Geo}, \dots, D_M^{Geo}, D_1^{SVD}, D_2^{SVD}, \dots, D_M^{SVD} \right)$$

eq(2.20)

Based on the distances $D_{Fusion} = (d_1, d_2, \dots, d_M)$, the minimum distances classifier is active to complete the Required task .

3.3.1 Modify Manhattan Distance Measure

The measurement is modified and is used as being based on the geometric features of the object and was incorporated with standard division to give better results and closer to reality. An image hybrid measure is proposed for assessing the similarity among grey-scale images. The new measure that is called MMDM is used as a combination of two parts The first part is based on geometry method and the second part is represented by standard division . The first part uses the concept of Manhattan distance geometry theoretic based. The new measure takes advantages of both statistical and geometrical features. New hybrid image dependent measure with better result than statistical measure is proposed. The new measure is robust with   significant noise. The new measure outperforms SSIM in detecting image similarity at low PSNR with Gaussian noise, with nearly 80% increase in performance. Figure (3.8) explained the algorithm of proposed method.

Algorithm(5) The first proposed measurement MMDM
Input: x which are the observed image and y are the saved image
Output: r similarity value range of the measure lies between 0 and 1.
Step 1: Convert image values into double type. *Step 2: set(p)=Manhattan distance(x ,y)* *Eq//(2.19)* *Step 3: set(q)= standard deviation (y)* *Eq//(1.1)* *Step 4: compute Z* *Z= (p / q)^2* *Step 5: 1- minimum distance* *Step 6: perform the comparisons (evaluate the results)* *End of Algorithm*

Figure(3.8) The first proposed measure for similarity

between faces   .

And the flow chart of the proposed measure will be as Figure(3.9)

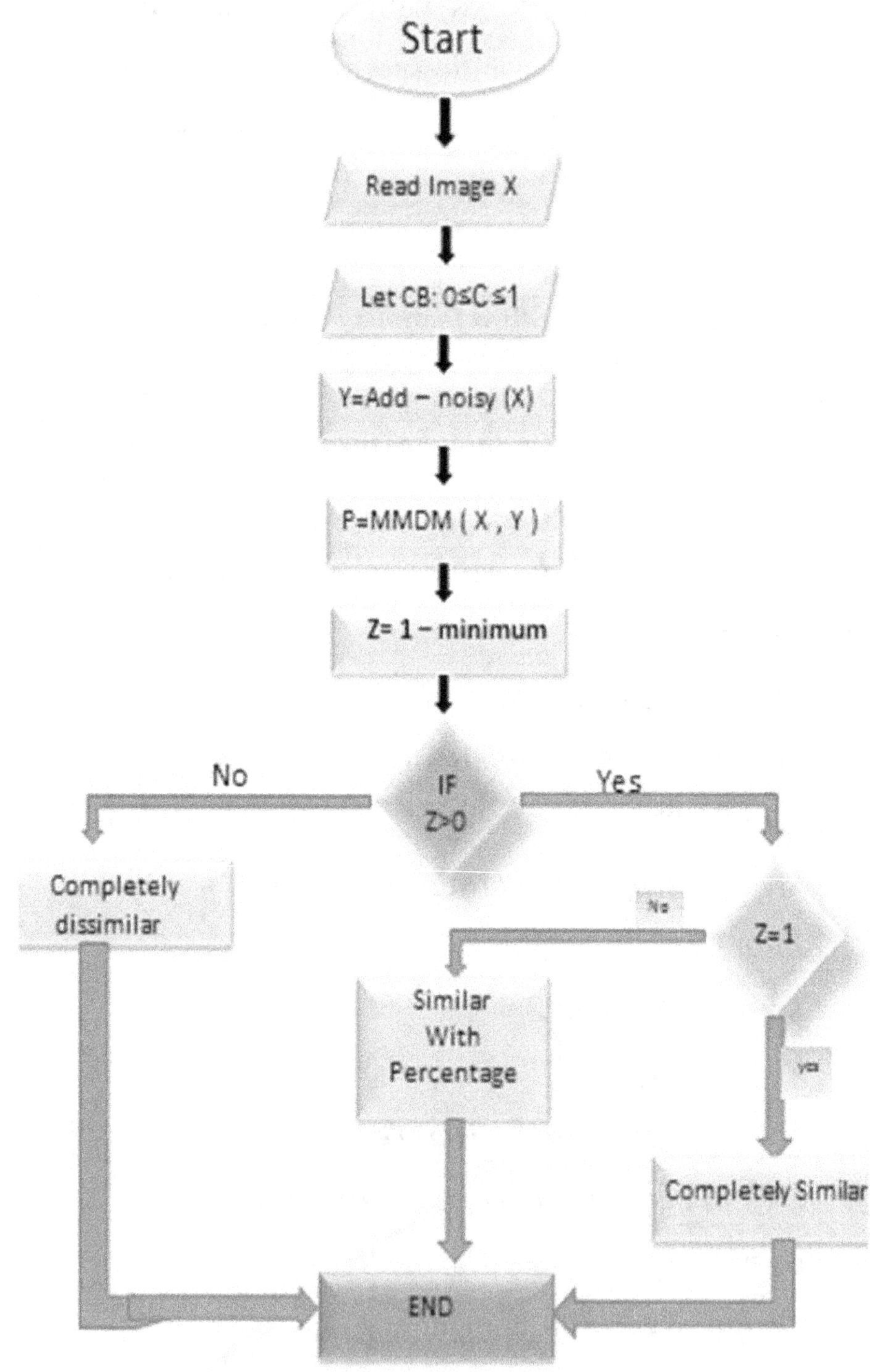

Figure (3-9) Flow chart of the proposed measure

3.5 Implementation of MMDM

Step1: Read an image

Let's take cropping-image of size (48*50) matrix

and call it y as in Figure (3-3)

Step2: Read the noisy image (with Gaussian noise)

Let y be the noisy version of x with 30 dB PSNR

 Step3:compute the geometric features as follow

1- Determine four point in the cropped image of

the observed image. As explained in Table(3-1)

Table (3-1) shows the of value of canter point of the IOR

features selected images

ROI	Coordinates	
	X	Y
Eye right	69.50 00	105
Eye left	1.205 00	98
Nose	96	1.30 500
Cente r	94.50 000	1.15 500

2- Compute the Euclidian distance between the each point and other points and the angles between the center and points the eyes and nose point and

points the eyes we chive (12) distance. see table (3-2) and (2) angles as following:

The point $P_0 P_1 P_2 P_3$

$$EU(P_0, P_1) = \sqrt{(x_0 - x_1)^2 + (y_0 - y_1)^2}$$

$$(2\text{-}16)$$

Table (3-) shows the of value of 12 distance between each point to others

Distance	value	Distance	value	Distance	value	Distance	value
P_0 $\_P_1$	3 1.340 86	P_1 $\_P_0$	1 5.074 81	P_2 $\_P_0$	2 7.115 45	P_3 $\_P_0$	5.0 74813
P_0 $\_P_2$	2 7.115 49	P_1 $\_P_2$	7 7635 10	P_2 $\_P_1$	5 1.478 15	P_3 $\_P_1$	4 0.70 012
P_0 $\_P_3$	4 0.700 12	P_1 $\_P_3$	3 1.340 86	P_2 $\_P_3$	5 1.478 15	P_3 $\_P_2$	36. 77635

The angles $t1$, $t2$

$$t = tan^{-1}(S_1 - S_2)/(1 + S_1 * S_2))$$

$$(2.19)$$

$t1 = 1.45058 \qquad t2 = 2.1515$

Step5 :Compute the statistical features by SVD function.

Step6: Combine the geometric and statistic features by append function

Step7: Matching the features of tow image (saved ,observed) by the one of the proposed measure.

$$M = \left(\frac{\Sigma_{i=1}^{n} |x-y|}{std\ y}\right)^2$$

Step8: There are 19 distance ,certainly chose the minimum distance

 min= 0.00818

Step9 : Subtract the minimum distance from 1 as

1-0.00818=**0.99181**

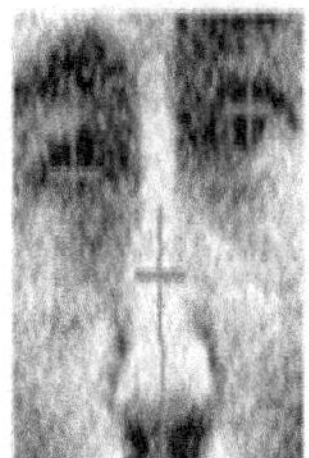

observed image(x)   gray level(x)

saved image(y)

Figure (3-9): Graph showing the final step of proposed measures with the counter for images similarities .

3.3.2 Modify Euclidean Distance Measure

Modify Euclidean distance for being new measurement for similarity between images because it is dependent on geometric features of object to give better results and closer to reality . Details are below, these procedure described in algorithm (6) ,see Figure (3.9).

Algorithm(6)The second proposed similarity measurement MEDM
Input: x which are the observed vector and y are the stored vector
Output: r similarity value range of the measure lies between 0 and 1.

Step 1: Convert image values into double type.

Step 2: set(p)=Euclidian distance(x ,y)   Eq//(2.1)

Step 3: set(q)= $\sum y^2$

Step 4: compute Z

$$Z= C*(P/q)$$

Step 5: 1- minimum distance

Step 6: perform the comparisons (evaluate the results)

End of Algorithm

Figure(3.10) the second proposed measure for similarity between images .

And the flow chart of the proposed measure will be as figure(3.11).

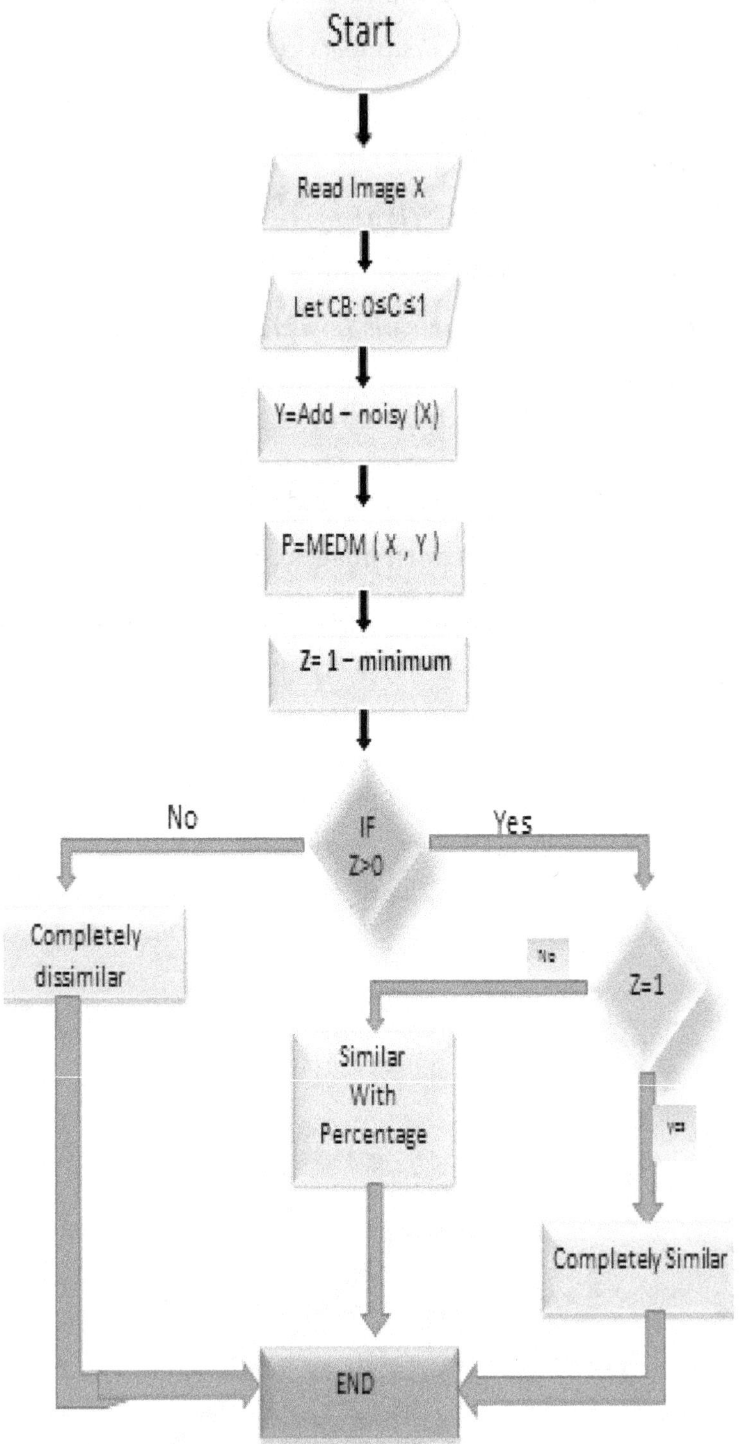

Figure (3-11) Flow chart of the proposed measure

3.5 Implementation of MEDM

Step1: Input an image

Let's take cropping-image of size (48*50) matrix
and call it y as in Figure (3-3)

Step2: Read the noisy image (with Gaussian noise)
Let y be the noisy version of x with 30 dB PSNR

Step3:compute the geometric features as follow
1- Determine four point in the cropped image of
the observed image.as explained in table (3-1)

Table (3-1) shows the of value of canter point of the IOR
features selected images.

IOR	Coordinates	
	X	Y
Eye right	69.50 00	105
Eye left	1.205 00	98
Nose	96	1.30 500
Cente r	94.50 000	1.15 500

2- Compute the euclidian distance between the
each point and another points and the angles between
the center and points the eyes and nose point and
points the eyes we will chive (12) distance(see table
(3-2) and (2) angles as folloing:
The point $P_0 P_1 P_2 P_3$
$EU(P_0, P_1)$

$$= \sqrt{(x_0 - x_1)^2 + (y_0 - y_1)^2} \qquad (2.1)$$

Table (3-2) shows the of value of 12 distance between

canter point to others

Distance	value	Distance	value	Distance	value	Distance	value
$P_0\_P_1$	31.34086	$P_1\_P_0$	15.07481	$P_2\_P_0$	27.11545	$P_3\_P_0$	5.074813
$P_0\_P_2$	27.11549	$P_1\_P_2$	7763510	$P_2\_P_1$	51.47815	$P_3\_P_1$	40.70012
$P_0\_P_3$	40.70012	$P_1\_P_3$	31.34086	$P_2\_P_3$	51.47815	$P_3\_P_2$	36.77635

The angles $t1,\ t2$

$$t1 = tan^{-1}(S_1 - S_2)/(1 + S_1 * S_2)) \qquad (2.8)$$

$t1 = 1.45058 \qquad t1 = 2.15153$

Step5 :Compute the statstical features by SVD function.

Step6: Combaine the geometric and statistic features by append function

Step7: Matching the features of tow image (saved ,observed) by the one of the proposed measure.

$$E = C * \left(\frac{\sum_{i=1}^{n} \left(\sqrt{xi - yi} \right)^2}{y} \right)^2$$

Step8: There are 19 distance ,certainly chose the minimum distance

 min= 0.00818

Step9 :   Subtract the minimum distance from 1 as

min = 1.99029

1- 0.0011 = **0.9999**

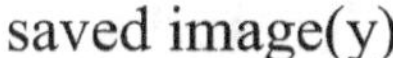

observed image(x)   gray level(x)

saved image(y)

Figure (3-10): Graph showing the final step of proposed measures with the counter for images similarities .

4.1 Introduction

This chapter discusses the simulation of the proposed measures, which are presented in Chapter Three. Comparisons are made between the proposed measures, and the standard and existing measures. The proposed measures are implemented by using Mat lab programming language. The experimental results are analyzed to illustrate the results.

The proposed measures are simulated and tested with Gaussian noise, which is the most popular source of noise encountered in signal processing systems. Human face images a data base face94 are considered.

4.2 Dataset Description

Faces94 Database: This face image database is produced at University of Essex. Faces94 database is includes 152 distinguishing persons (19 females and 133 males)for any one20 images . Each image of a person has significant changes in appearance, location and head. The size of each image is (180×200) with RGB color. Figure (4.1) shows samples faces from this database.

Many of Experiments are performed on images from Faces94 face database, the images are chosen randomly from which only 80 persons are chosen randomly, from the twenty images of each person only one image was used for observed image, and

the remaining nineteen images are saved.

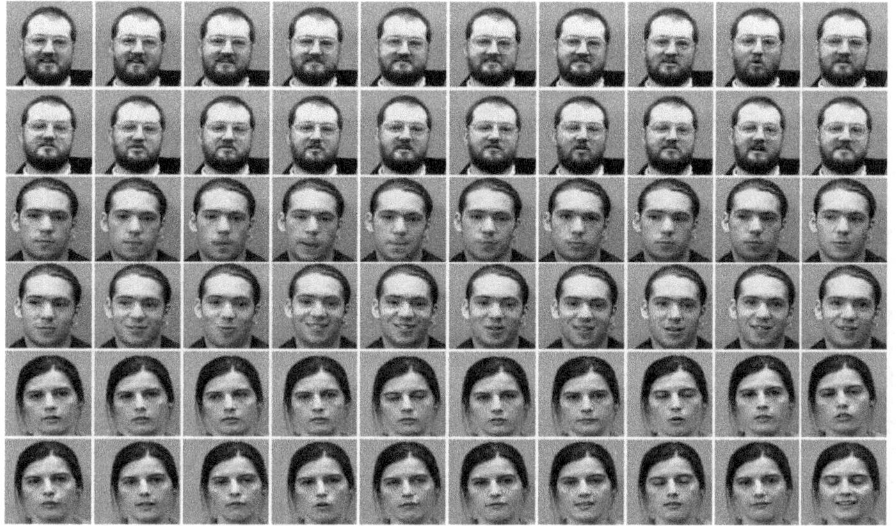

Figure (4.1): Some sample images from the Faces94 database.

4-3 sample of feature vector.

In the table(4.1) there are numbers of features extracted from the image that has 35 features combined between two parts only . The first part is the geometrical features of distance (12) Euclidean distance and angles (2 angles).In the second part statistical features are represented by the SVD method which has 21 features that mean the vector of each image has 35 features.

Table (4-1) shows the of value features extracted from three

Type of features	Image1	Image2	Image3
	25.495	24.186	27.771
	13.086	13.647	14.318
	28.901	28.57	32.33
	25.495	45.136	53.339
	36.335	28.57	32.33
Distances between any two points that have been chosen in face.	44.071	36.401	39.513
	44.071	24.187	27.771
	28.901	34.34	37.911
	36.173	45.136	53.339
	36.335	34.34	37.911
	13.086	13.647	14.318
	36.173	36.401	39.513
angles	24.214	35.053	36.721
	- 2.748	3.085-	1.963
SVD features	-9.437	2.401	-3.109

- 7.652	1.707	-3.109
10.892	10.696	9.619
-1.147	10.696	9.619
6.939	8.347	5.829
2.869	-8.035	1.561
4.611	7.01	7.237
3.572	-3.161	-5.048
3.180	-8.708	1.639
- 3.608	9.246	2.322
-4.108	-2.685	-4.559
-3.507	-1.422	3.293
1.124	-3.764	1.693
-9.159	-1.605	4.666
-3.209	2.054	7.373
-3.209	2.054	7.373
-3.088	-1.346	6.072
9.539	5.412	1.867
2.429	3.574	4.961
1.307	1.383	1.52
1.886	2.049	2.181

4.4 Modify Manhattan Distance Measure

The proposed measure is compared with SSIM as in Figures (4-2). The comparison is performed with Gaussian noise which is the most popular image noise. The proposed measure gives a great throughput and best results when working on human face images as shown Table (4-2).

Figure 4-2 shows that the blue block a new measure is located on the right side of the red and black curves belonging to SSIM and MDM, respectively (this means that MMDM outperforms SSIM with 97% And MDM no results .MMDM is able to detect similarity with Gaussian noise with any ratio of PSNR where SSIM and MDM fail.

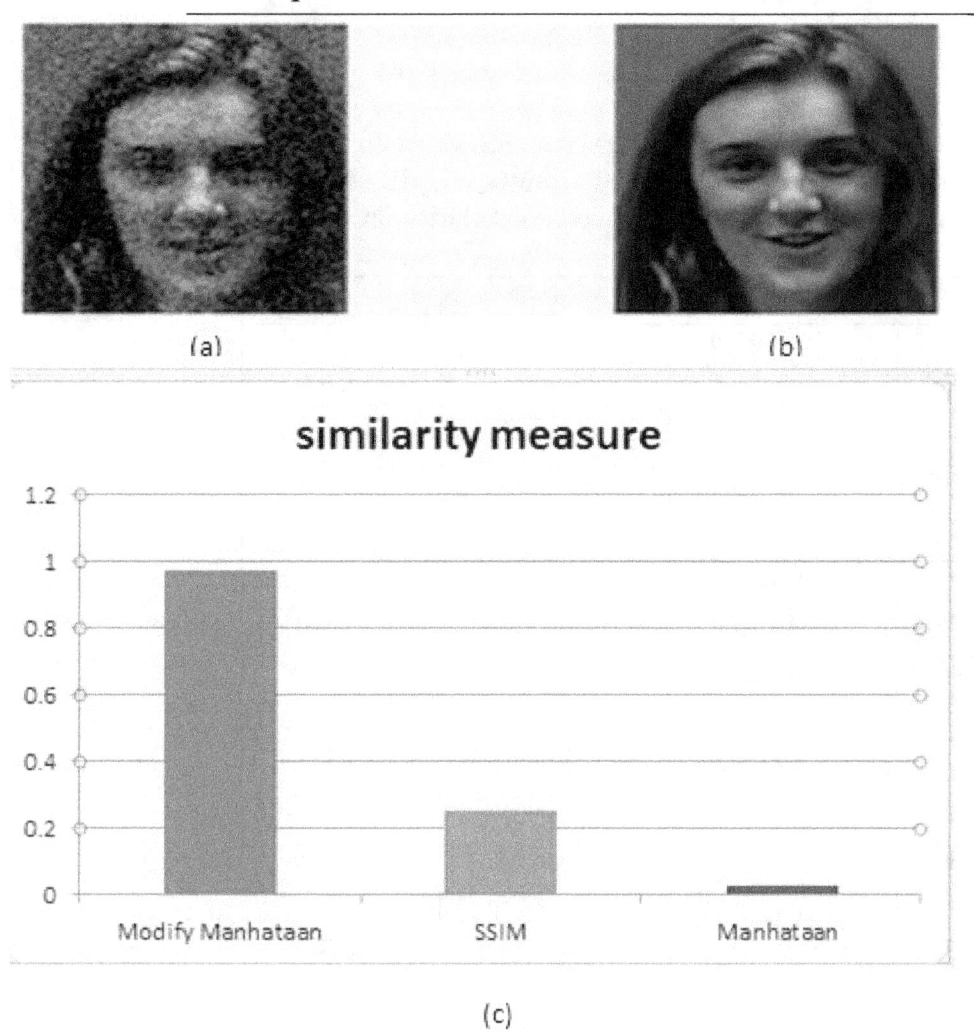

Figure (4-2)Performance Comparison of SSIM ,MDM ,and MMDM using different images. (human face) with Gaussian noise..(a) observed image, noisy image , (b)Saved image (c): Comparison of MMDM,MDM and SSIM.

TABLE 4-2 Proposed MMDM vs. SSIM with different Gaussian noise degree that graded from(0– 65)dB. It can be notice that MMDM is able to detect similarity in different PSNR.

PSNR	SSIM	MMDM	SJHS
5	0.020216	0.98587	0.5934
10	0.041481	0.98644	0.9354
15	0.08826	0.98892	0.9604
20	0.16850	0.99182	0.961
25	0.28499	0.99241	0.9607
30	0.42458	0.99152	0.9617
35	0.53275	0.99200	0.9645
40	0.58830	0.99213	0.9694
45	0.60957	0.99206	0.9773
50	0.61707	0.99210	0.9877
55	0.61962	0.99212	0.9969
60	0.62074	0.99210	0.9999
65	0.62103	0.99210	1

In Table 4-2, is noticed that MMDM reaches the maximum similarity when the PSNR=30dB approximately, and SSIM reaches maximum similarity with PSNR 65dB.Also it can be noticed that SSIM decreasing when PSNR increasing while MMDM is still able to detect the similarity and it gives similarity about 100% with the same PSNR.

Table (4-4) Proposed MEDM VS. SSIM, EDM and CHE with Gaussian noise PSNR=30dB.

IM AGE	MM DM	M DM	C HE	SS IM
Image1	0.99 24	0.5 826	0.6 516	0.4 507
Image2	0.96 31	2.2 -225	0.4 718	0.4 108
Image3	0.94 57	3.5 -205	0.3 610	0.3 788
Image4	0.84 67	0.8 199	0.8 420	0.5 275
Image5	0.99 99	0.8 017	0.9 180	0.5 890
Image6	0.99 99	0.8 485	0.9 114	0.5 851
Image7	0.99 99	0.8 115	0.8 932	0.5 799
Image8	0.96 68	2.2 -823	0.6 285	0.3 157
Image9	0.92 11	4.1 -803	0.1 235	0.4 714
Image10	0.97 37	-1.8769	0.5 052	0.2 363
Image11	0.93 19	-3.6201	0.2 932	0.3 498
Image12	0.94 21	-3.4546	0.5 001	0.2 476
Image13	0.94 62	-2.9811	0.4 707	0.3 359

Image14	0.9373	-3.6002	0.3146	0.1792
Image15	0.9557	-2.7924	0.4599	0.4231
Image16	0.9318	-3.0157	0.4664	0.3074
Image17	0.8964	-4.1972	0.0031	0.4344
Image18	0.9362	-3.5667	0.0705	0.2260
Image19	0.9272	-3.3514	0.2364	0.4519
Image20	0.9043	-4.3667	0.9033	0.3191
Image21	0.9302	-3.5615	0.3301	0.4528
Image 22	0.9489	-3.2468	0.4884	0.4136
Image23	0.9452	3.1-816	0.5003	0.4170
Image24	0.9446	-3.1384	0.3057	0.3599
Image25	0.9234	4.1-507	0.2419	0.4966

Figure (4-5): Graph showing the comparison of the
measures with same PSNR

4.5 Modify Euclidian Distance Measure

(MEDM) measure, outperforms existing
distance-based measures in detecting image similarity
at low PSNR with Gaussian noise, nearly 100%
increase in performance.

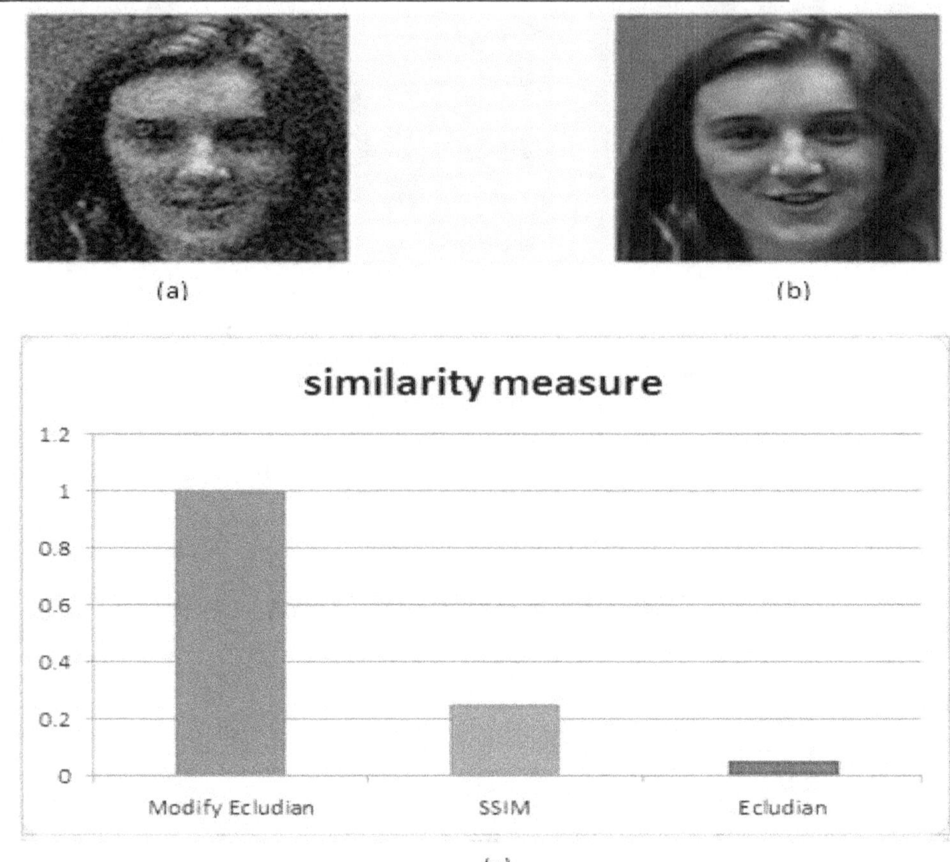

Figure (4-3) Performance Comparison of SSIM ,EDM,and MEDM using different images (human face) with Gaussian noise..(a) observed image, noisy image , (b)Saved image (c): Comparison of SSIM, EDM and MEDM.

In Figures (4-3), it is shown the that the blue column which belongs to (new similarity) is on the right side of the red and black column which belongs to Euclidian distance and SSIM respectively ,and that means that MEDM outperform SSIM with at least 99% and EDM with 20%. MEDM is able to detect similarity under low PSNR (significant noise) where the SSIM and EDM decreased .

TABLE (4-3) The extended comparison of new measure MEDM vs. SSIM with different Gaussian noise degree that graded from (0 – 65). It can be noticed that (MEDM) is able to detect similarity in any degree of PSNR .

PSNR	SSIM	MEDM	S JHS
0	0.01108	1	0.5934
5	0.02204	1	0.8134
10	0.04299	1	0.9354
15	0.08820	1	0.9604
20	0.167300	1	0.961
25	0.28524	1	0.9607
30	0.42616	1	0.9617
35	0.53466	1	0.9645
40	0.58846	1	0.9694
45	0.60960	1	0.9773
50	0.61704	1	0.9877
55	0.61956	1	0.9969
60	0.62068	1	0.9999
65	0.62102	1	1

In Table (3-4) it can be noticed that (MEDM) is able to detect similarity in any degree of PSNR .

Also it can be noticed that performance SSIM is decreasing when PSNR is increasing by 5 dB while (new measure) is still able to detect the similarity and it gave similarity about 100% with the different PSNR. Also it is noted that MEDM reaches the maximum similarity (approximately similar equal to

1) when the PSNR increase from (0 - 65)dB while SSIM reach maximum similarity when the PSNR=65 dB. The comparison is performed with Gaussian noise. As for the hybrid measure (SJHS) it detects similarity and under the same conditions, but the new measure (MEDM) outperforms in performance. The result of comparing the proposed measure with SSIM is shown in Figures (4-3) .

TABLE (4-4) PROPOSED MEDM VS. SSIM, EDM and CHE with GAUSSIAN NOISE PSNR=30dB.

IMAGE	MEDM	EDM	CHE	SSIM
Image 1	1.0000	0.3190	0.6516	0.4507
Image 2	1.0000	0.1144 -	0.4718	0.4108
Image 3	1.0000	0.3885 -	0.3610	0.3788
Image 4	1.0000	0.8336	0.8420	0.5275
Image 5	1.0000	0.9284	0.9180	0.5890
Image 6	1.0000	0.8613	0.9114	0.5851
Image 7	1.0000	0.8654	0.8932	0.5799
Image 8	1.0000	0.0187	0.6285	0.3157
Image 9	1.0000	0.6950	0.1235	0.4714

Image 10	1.0000	0.0072	0.5052	0.2363
Image 11	1.000	0.5347	0.2932	0.3498
Image 12	1.0000	0.3739	0.5001	0.2476
Image 13	1.0000	0.2902	0.4707	0.3359
Image 14	1.0000	0.4258	0.3146	0.1792
Image 15	1.0000	0.1916	0.4599	0.4231
Image 16	1.0000	0.2463	0.4664	0.3074
Image 17	0.9999	0.7595	0.0031	0.4344
Image 18	1.0000	0.5697	0.0705	0.2260
Image 19	0.9999	0.5227	0.2364	0.4519
Image 20	0.9999	1.0996	0.9033	0.3191
Image 21	1.0000	0.4756	0.3301	0.4528
Image 22	1.0000	0.3334	0.4884	0.4136
Image 23	1.0000	0.3024 -	0.5003	0.4170
Image 24	1.0000	0.3703	0.3057	0.3599
Image 25	1.0000	0.4928	0.2419	0.4966

In Table (4-4), it is noticed that MEDM outperforms SSIM and EDM and shows that maximum performance increasing with SSIM happens when PSNR is 10 and with EDM when PSNR is 0.

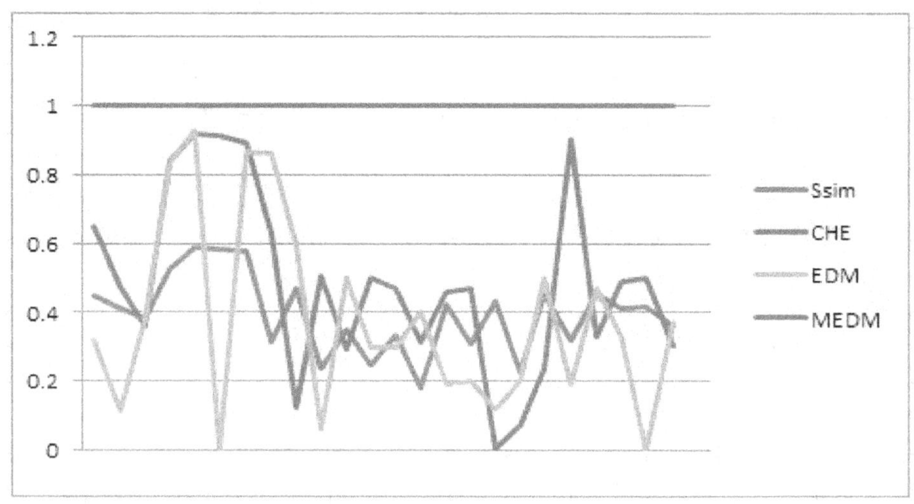

Figure (4-5): Graph showing the comparison of the measures with same PSNR

4.5 Measurement A Accuracy

The result from two measures (MMDM,MEDM) in training stage where the training with database of 1600 and the result has a different similarity rate, as shown in Table(4.6) and Figure (4.8) by using the following equation:

$$Accuracy = (TP + TN)/(TP + FP + FN + TN)$$

Where *TP* Contains True Positives that properly similarity positive states ; *FP* is False Positives that improperly similarity negative situations, *TN* is True Negative that properly similarity negative states and

FN is False Negative that is improperly similarity positive states .

Table (4.7):shown the difference between two measures rate

Experiment No.	No. of image	Efficiency of MEDM	Efficiency of MMDM	Efficiency of MDM	Efficiency of EDM
1stexperiment	100	100%	96%	20%	26%
2ndexperiment	100	100%	97%	40%	37%
3thexperiment	100	99%	98%	33%	38%
4thexperiment	100	97%	95%	35%	40%
5thexperiment	100	98%	90%	39%	40%

Chapter Five

Conclusions and Future work

5.1 Introduction

A new image similarity measures called(Modify Manhattan and modify Euclidean distances) are proposed. The new measures are tested with a face data bace and compared with structural similarity (SSIM)measure, the conclusion can be described by the following :

1. The modification of the Euclidean distance that is used for computing the matching feature vector is better than others metrics such as

(Euclidean distance, Manhattan distance, chebychev distance) gives lesser accuracy .(see Appendix B)

2. The proposed measures provide improved performance (more similarity) under weighty noise than the existing statistical-based measure SSIM .(see section 4.4)

3. A new area has been used the local level in this work.

4. The proposed measures (MMDM and MEDM) increase the confidence to least 98% than traditional   and at least 85-90 % than SSIM.(see section 4.4 and section 4.5)

5. Through our experiments in this work, we know that the hybrid features (statistical and geometrical) are the best types of features known   as color, shape, histogram …etc).

6. Gaussian noise does not pose a threat to similarity measures based on geometrical features.

5.2 Future Work

In this work, we focus on geometrical similarity measures based on a new definition of

Manhattan and Euclidian distance . Some new directions are possible:

1. The proposed measures can be active in many pattern recognition systems such as iris recognition, hand ,foot and other.
2. The proposed measures can be supported by correlation , between the two images .
3. The above measures can be further improved by , using system with video camera.
4. We can develop measures to detect the similarity of 3-D images.

[1] *Nikvand, N., & Wang, Z.(2010) **Generic image similarity based on Kolmogorov complexity**. " International Conference on Image Processing.*

[2] *Wang, Z., & Bovik, A. C. (2006). **Modern image quality assessment.** Synthesis Lectures on Image, Video, and Multimedia Processing, 2(1), 1-156.,2006*

[3]*Wang, Z., Bovik, A. C., Sheikh, H. R., & Simoncelli, E. P. (2004). **Image quality assessment: from error visibility to structural similarity**. IEEE transactions on image processing, 13(4), 600-612*

[4] *Simini, F., Anfodillo, T., Carrer, M., Banavar, J. R., & Maritan, A. (2010). **Self-similarity and scaling in forest communities**. Proceedings of the National Academy of Sciences, 107(17), 7658-7662*

[5] *Goshtasby, A. A. (2012). **Image registration**: Principles, tools and methods. Springer Science & Business Media*

[6]*George, A., & Livingston, S. J. (2013). **A survey on full reference image quality assessment algorithms.** International*

Journal of Research in Engineering and Technology, 2(12), 303-307.

[7] *Altufaili, F. M., Mohammed, H. R., & Hussain, Z. M. (2016).* ***A Noise-Resistant Hybrid Measure for Images Similarity.***

[8] *Hassan, A. F., Cailin, D., & Hussain, Z. M. (2014).* ***An information-theoretic image quality measure:*** *Comparison with statistical similarity.*

[9] *Spatz, C. (2007).* ***Basic statistics****: Tales of distributions. Cengage Learning*

[10] *Shi, L. (2007).* ***Health services research methods****. Cengage Learning.*

[11] *R. Vallejos, D. Mancilla and J. Acosta(2016)* ***"Image similarity assessment based on coefficients of spatial association,"*** *Springer-Journal of Mathematical Imaging and Vision.*

[12] *Premaratne, P., & Premaratne, M. (2012).* ***New structural similarity measure for image comparison****. In International Conference on Intelligent Computing (pp. 292-297). Springer, Berlin, Heidelberg.*

[13] *Soundararajan, R., & Bovik, A. C. (2013).* ***Survey of information theory in visual quality assessment. Signal,*** *Image and Video Processing, 7(3), 391-401*

[14] *Kalinić, H., Lončarić, S., & Bijnens, B. (2011).* ***A novel image similarity measure for image registration****. In 2011 7th International Symposium on Image and Signal Processing and Analysis (ISPA) (pp. 195-199).*

[15] Sugiyama, M., & Borgwardt, K. M. (2013). **Measuring statistical dependence via the mutual information dimension.** In Twenty-Third International Joint Conference on Artificial Intelligence.

[16]Lu, X., Zhang, S., Su, H., & Chen, Y. (2008). **Mutual information-based multimodal image registration using a novel joint histogram estimation.** Computerized Medical Imaging and Graphics, 32(3), 202-209

[17]Farooque, M. A., & Rohankar, J. S. (2013). **Survey on various noises and techniques for denoising the color image.** International Journal of Application or Innovation in Engineering & Management (IJAIEM), 2(11), 217-221

[18]Bianco, S., Ciocca, G., Marini, F., & Schettini, R. (2009). **Image quality assessment by preprocessing and full reference model combination.** In Image Quality and System Performance VI. International Society for Optics and Photonics.

[19] Hore, A., & Ziou, D. (2010). **Image quality metrics: PSNR vs. SSIM.** In 2010 20th International Conference on Pattern Recognition (pp. 2366-2369).

[20]Wang, Z., & Bovik, A. C. (2002). **A universal image quality index.** signal processing letters, 9(3), 81-84.

[21]Reisenhofer, R., Bosse, S., Kutyniok, G., & Wiegand, T. (2018). **A Haar wavelet-based perceptual similarity index for image quality assessment.** Signal Processing: Image Communication, 61, 33-43

[22] Wang, Z., & Bovik, A. C. (2009). **Mean squared error: Love it or leave it**? A new look at signal fidelity measures. IEEE signal processing magazine, 26(1), 98-117.

[23] Lehmann, E. L., & Casella, G. (2006). **Theory of point estimation**. Springer Science & Business Media.

[24] Huynh-Thu, Q., & Ghanbari, M. (2008). **Scope of validity of PSNR in image/video quality assessment. Electronics letters,** 44(13), 800-801.

[25] Hore, A., & Ziou, D. (2010). **Image quality metrics: PSNR vs. SSIM**. In 2010 20th International Conference on Pattern Recognition (pp. 2366-2369). IEEE.

[26] Mitra, S., & Gofman, M. (Eds.). (2016). **Biometrics in a Data Driven World**: Trends, Technologies, and Challenges. CRC Press

[27] Jain, A. K., Ross, A., & Prabhakar, S. (2004). **An introduction to biometric recognition.** Transactions on circuits and systems for video technology, 14(1), 4-20.

[28]   Asit Kumar Datta, Madhura Datta and Pradipta Kumar Banerjee,(2016) **"Face Detection and Recognition Theory and Practice"**, Book, Taylor & Francis Group, LLC.

[29] Heitmeyer, R. (2000). **Biometric identification promises fast and secure processing of airline passengers.** ICAO journal, 55(9), 10-11.

[30] Salam J. Edan (2017)''**A Hybrid Approach to Human Face Recognition based on SVD and Gabor filters**'',M.Sc. Thesis, Thi-qar Univercity, Collage of

Euducation for pure science, Department of computer Science,Iraq,

[31]Jain, A. K., & Li, S. Z. (2011). ***Handbook of face recognition*** *. New York: springer.book*

[32] ***"What is Facial Recognition? Definition from Techopedia".*** *(2018)Techopedia.com.*

[33] Ambre, S., Masurekar, M., & Gaikwad, S. (2019). ***Face Recognition Using Raspberry PI****. In Modern Approaches in Machine Learning and Cognitive Science: A Walkthrough (pp. 1-11). Springer, Cham.*

[34]Huang, T., Xiong, Z., & Zhang, Z. (2005). ***Face recognition applications****. In Handbook of Face Recognition (pp. 371-390). Springer, New York, NY.*

[35]Kubota, Y. (2017). ***Apple iPhone X Production Woe Sparked by Juliet and Her Romeo****. The Wall Street Journal*

[36] ***"China bets on facial recognition in big drive for total surveillance".*** *Washington Post. 2018. Retrieved 23 February 2019.*

[37]Sarsoh, J. T., & Hashem, K. M. (2012). ***Classifying of human face images based on the graph theory concepts****. Global Journal of Computer Science and Technology.*

[38]Sampat, M. P., Wang, Z., Gupta, S., Bovik, A. C., & Markey, M. K. (2009). ***Complex wavelet structural similarity****: A new image similarity index. IEEE transactions on image processing, 18(11), 2385-2401.*

[39] Wang, H., Maldonado, D., & Silwal, S. (2011). *A nonparametric-test-based structural similarity measure for digital images.* Computational statistics & data analysis, 55(11), 2925-2936.

[40]Hassan, A. F., Cailin, D., & Hussain, Z. M. (2014). *An information-theoretic image quality measure:* Comparison with statistical similarity.

[41] S.K.Ali and Z.M. Aydam,(2019), *"Gestures conversion to Arabic letters* .

[42] Face94 (1994) L. Spacek, University of essex, department of computer science, http://cswww.

[43]Mitra, S., & Gofman, M. (Eds.). (2016). *Biometrics in a Data Driven World*: Trends, Technologies, and Challenges. CRC Press

[44]Vijayakumari, V. (2013). *Face recognition techniques*: A survey. World journal of computer application and technology, 1(2), 41-50.

[45]Dougherty, G. (2012). *Pattern recognition and classification*: an introduction. Springer Science & Business Media.

[46]5Park, U. (2009). *Face Recognition: face in video, age invariance, and facial marks.* Michigan State University. Department of Computer Science.

[47]Hamid M. Hasan*, "Human Face Recognition using Hybrid Techniques"*,(2012) Ph.D. dissertation, Electrical Eng. Dept.

[48] Gül, A. B. (2003). **Holistic face recognition by dimension reduction** (Master's thesis).

[49] Mohammed, A. A., Minhas, R., Wu, Q. J., & Sid-Ahmed, M. A. (2011). **Human face recognition based on multidimensional PCA and extreme learning machine.** Pattern Recognition, 44, 2588-2597.

[50] Arubas, E. (2013). **Face detection and recognition** (Theory and Practice). OpenCV.

[51] Umbaugh, S. E. (2010). **Digital image processing and analysis: human and computer vision applications with CVIPtools.** CRC press.

[52] Some sample images from the local database(2019).

[53] Gonzalez, R. C., Woods, R. E., & Eddins, S. L. (2004). **Digital image processing using MATLAB.** Pearson Education India.

[54] Lewis, M. B., & Ellis, H. D. (2003). **How we detect a face: A survey of psychological evidence. International Journal of Imaging Systems and Technology,** 13(1), 3-7

[55] Viraktamath, S. V., Katti, M., Khatawkar, A., & Kulkarni, P. (2013). **Face detection and tracking using OpenCV.** The SIJ Transactions on Computer Networks & Communication Engineering (CNCE), 1(3), 45-50.

[56] AL-Dulami, M. A. M. (2005). **Feature-Based Face Recognition System Using Gabor Filter (Doctoral dissertation,** M. Sc Thesis, Department of Computer Sciences of the University of Technology).

[57]Deza, M. M., & Deza, E. (2009). **Encyclopedia of distances**. In Encyclopedia of distances (pp. 1-583). Springer, Berlin, Heidelberg.

[58]Clapham, C., & Nicholson, J. (2009). **Oxford Concise Dictionary of Mathematics, Gradient. PDF).** Addison-Wesley, 348.**Mathematics"**, OUP oxford,2009.

[59]   A. H. Stroud, " **Approximate Calculation of Multiple Integrals"**, Prentice-HStenger, F. (1973). Approximate Calculation of Multiple Integrals (AH Stroud). SIAM Review, 15(1), 234.all Inc., Englewood Cli_s, N. J.,1971.

[60]   Dr Yeap Ban Har,Dr Joseph Yeo,Teh Keng Seng,Loh Cheng Yee,Ivy Chow,Neo Chai Meng and Jacinth Liew ,(2018) **"New Syllabus Mathematics   Teacher's Resource Book1"**,7th edition,OXFORD UNIVERSITY Press,.

[61]Greenwood, D. T. (2006). **Advanced dynamics**. Cambridge University Press.

[62]Kopetz, H. (2011).**Real-time systems: design principles for distributed embedded applications.** Springer Science & Business Media.

[63]Nguyen, H. T., & Rogers, G. S. (1989). **Fundamentals of mathematical statistics: Probability for statistics.** Springer Science & Business Media.

[64]Cao, D., & Yang, B. (2010, February). **An improved face recognition algorithm based on SVD.** In 2010 The 2nd

International Conference on Computer and Automation Engineering (ICCAE) (pp. 109-112). IEEE.

[65]Satonkar Suhas, S., Kurhe Ajay, B., & Khanale Prakash, B. ***Face Recognition Using Singular Value Decomposition of Facial Color Image Database.***2015.

[66]Sergios Theodoridis And Konstantinos Koutroumbas, ***"Pattern Recognition"***, Book, Elsevier Inc, 2009.

[67]Fukunaga, K. (2013). ***Introduction to statistical pattern recognition***. Elsevier.

[68]Barrah, E. M., Safi, S., & Malaoui, A. (2016). ***New Fusion of SVD and DCT-LBP for Face Recognition.***

[69]Mittal, R. K., & Garg, A.(2014)***Face Recognition through Combined SVD and LBP***. International Journal of Computer Applications, 975, 8887.

[70]Hong, Z. Q. (1991). ***Algebraic feature extraction of image for recognition***. Pattern recognition, 24(3), 211-219.

[71]Tian, Y., Tan, T., Wang, Y., & Fang, Y. (2003). ***Do singular values contain adequate information for face recognition?. Pattern recognition***, 36(3), 649-655.

[72]Pang, Y., Yu, N., Zhang, R., Rong, J., & Liu, Z. (2004). ***Fusion of SVD and LDA for face recognition.*** In 2004 International Conference on Image Processing, 2004. ICIP'04. (pp. 1417-1420). IEEE.

[73]Route De Soumaa, B. P. ***Score Fusion of SVD and DCT-RLDA for Face Recognition.***

[74] Yassin, D. H. P., Hoque, S., & Deravi, F. (2013). **Age Sensitivity of Face Recognition Algorithms.** In 2013 Fourth International Conference on Emerging Security Technologies (pp. 12-15).

[75] Verma, R., & Ali, J. (2013). **A comparative study of various types of image noise and efficient noise removal techniques.** International Journal of advanced research in computer science and software engineering, 3(10).

[76] Saxena, C., & Kourav, D. (2014). **Noises and image denoising techniques: a brief survey.** International journal of Emerging Technology and advanced Engineering, 4(3), 878-885.

[77] Agrawal, A., & Mishra, P. K. (2016). **Restoration and De-Noising of Digital Image Based on Non-Linear Diffusion Filter for Different Type of Noises.** International Journal of Engineering Science, 2608.

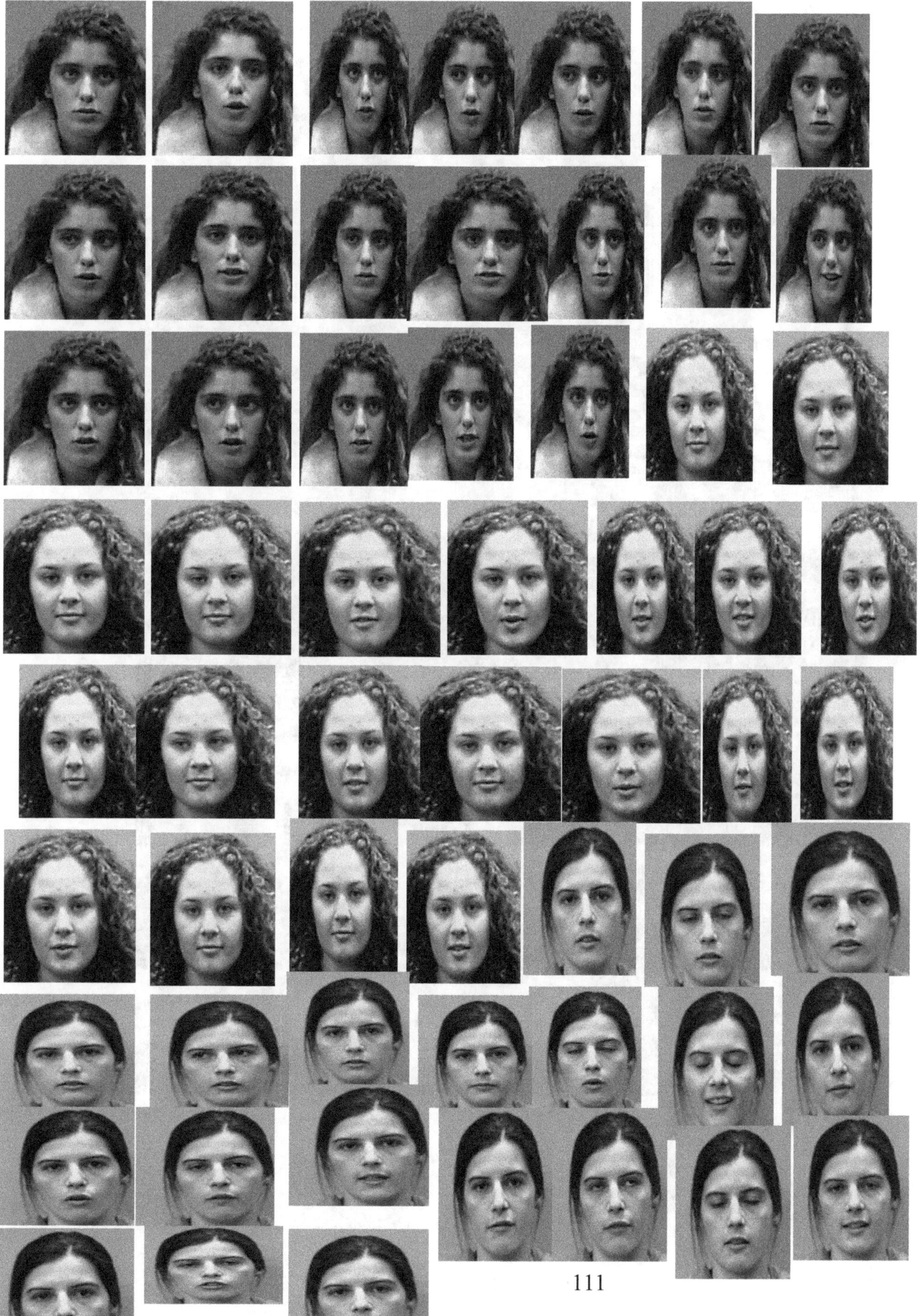

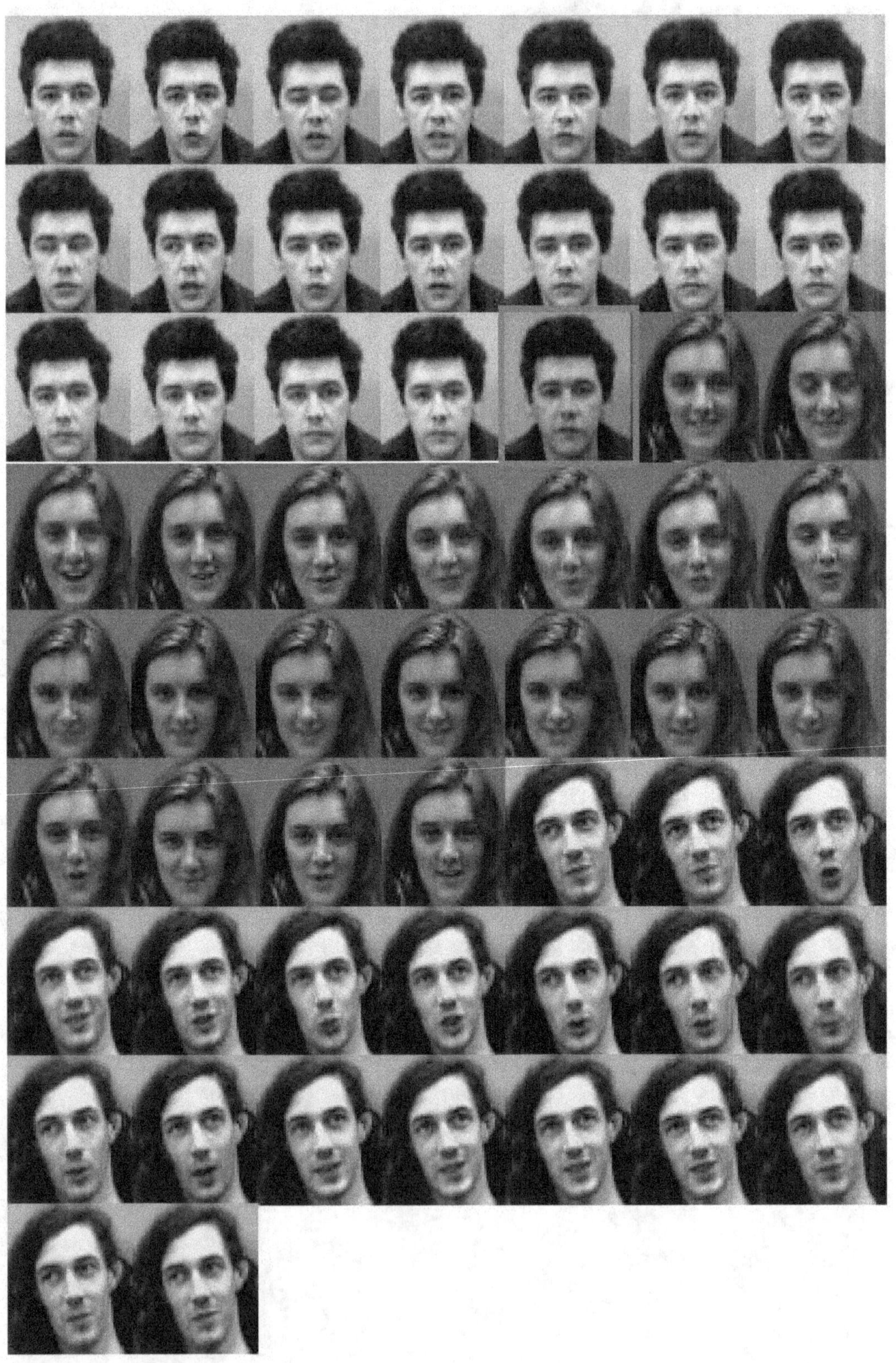

TABLE (4-6) comparison the proposed measures(MMDM,MEDM) VS.SSIM,EDM,CHE,MDM with Gaussian noise PSNR=30

IMAGE	MMDM	MEDM	MDM	EDM	CHE	SSIM
Image1	0.9924	1.0000	0.5826	0.3190	0.6516	0.4507
Image2	0.9631	1.0000	-2.2225	0.1144-	0.4718	0.4108
Image3	0.9457	1.0000	3.5205-	0.3885-	0.3610	0.3788
Image4	0.8467	1.0000	0.8199	0.8336	0.8420	0.5275
Image5	0.9999	1.0000	0.8017	0.9284	0.9180	0.5890
Image6	0.9999	1.0000	0.8485	0.8613	0.9114	0.5851
Image7	0.9999	1.0000	0.8115	0.8654	0.8932	0.5799
Image8	0.9668	1.0000	2.2823-	0.0187	0.6285	0.3157
Image9	0.9211	1.0000	4.1803-	0.6950-	0.1235	0.4714
Image10	0.9737	1.0000	1.8769-	0.0072-	0.5052	0.2363
Image11	0.9319	1.0000	3.6201-	0.5347-	0.2932	0.3498

		0				6
Image13	0.9462	1.0000	2.9811-	0.2902-	0.4707	0.3359
Image14	0.9373	1.0000	3.6002-	0.4258-	0.3146	0.1792
Image15	0.9557	1.0000	2.7924-	0.1916-	0.4599	0.4231
Image16	0.9318	1.0000	3.0157-	0.2463-	0.4664	0.3074
Image17	0.8964	0.9999	4.1972-	0.7595-	0.0031	0.4344
Image18	0.9362	1.0000	3.5667-	0.5697-	0.0705	0.2260
Image19	0.9272	0.9999	3.3514-	0.5227-	0.2364	0.4519
Image20	0.9043	0.9999	4.3667-	1.0996-	0.9033	0.3191
Image21	0.9302	1.0000	3.5615-	0.4756-	0.3301	0.4528
Image22	0.9489	1.0000	3.2468-	0.3334-	0.4884	0.4136
Image23	0.9452	1.0000	3.1816-	0.3024-	0.5003	0.4170
Image24	0.9446	1.0000	3.1384-	0.3703-	0.3057	0.3599
Image25	0.9234	1.0000	4.1507-	0.4928-	0.2419	0.4966

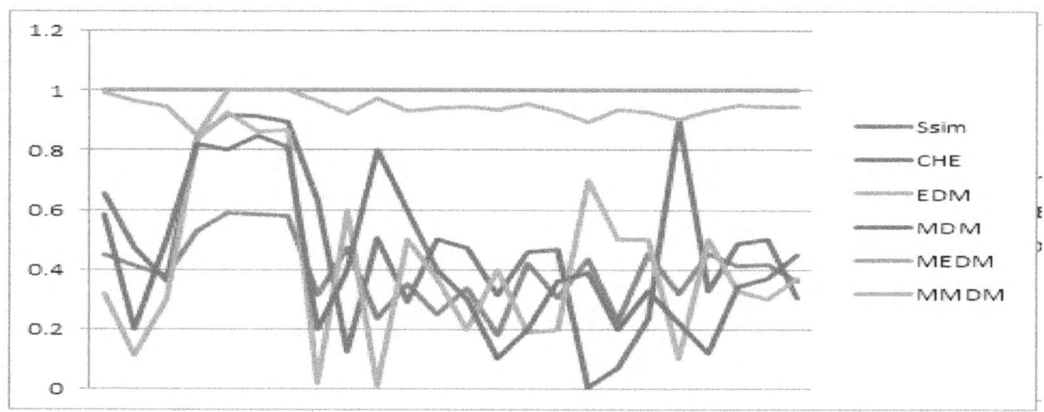

Figure (4.8)): Graph showing the comparison of the measures with same PSNR

References

.